The Boiling Pot of Injustice

Wounded By Cowardice!

—ɯ—

Kelvin D. Bodley

Copyright © 2006 by Kelvin D. Bodley

The Boiling Pot of Injustice
by Kelvin D. Bodley

Printed in the United States of America

ISBN 1-60034-178-0

All rights reserved solely by the author. The author guarantees all contents are original and do not infringe upon the legal rights of any other person or work. No part of this book may be reproduced in any form without the permission of the author. The views expressed in this book are not necessarily those of the publisher.

Unless otherwise indicated, Bible quotations are taken from the King James Version.

www.xulonpress.com

TABLE OF CONTENTS

PREFACE I
    Rev. Dr. Simon Bodley, Jr. xi

PREFACE II
    Rev. Dr. Jeremiah A. Wright, Jr. xv

PREDFACE III
    Dwight N. Randolph xix

Dedication
    Rev. Dr. Simon & Jenny Bodley xxi

Dedication
    Orange County Employees xxiii

Dedication
    Churches & Governmental Officials 29

Introduction
    Kelvin D. Bodley 31

Enslaved Freedom
    Chapter One 39

Walking Gracefully Through The Valley of The Shadow Of Employment Discrimination
    Chapter Two 47

Wounded By Cowardice
    Chapter Three 55

Just There
    Chapter Four 67

You Have A Right To Remain Silent In The Workplace
    Chapter Five 73

Hush, Somebody's Calling My Name
    Chapter Six 81

To Be Or Not To Be, That Is The Question?
    Chapter Seven 87

Fighting Employment Discrimination – Is The Lord On Your Side
    Chapter Eight 97

Thanks Lord, "I'll Take It From Here"!
    Chapter Nine 103

How To Prepare For A Legal Battle While On Your Job
    Chapter Ten 111

How Does One Determine If Their Legal Council Is Friend Or Foe? 115
    Chapter Eleven

Breaking Point
    Chapter Twelve..123

No Man Can Hinder Me
    Chapter Thirteen...133

Hello Lord, "Are You Still There"?
   Chapter Fourteen 139

Shout With A Victory
   Chapter Fifteen 147

Conclusion 153

Summary 157

Biography 159

Advertisement 161

Fourscore and seven years ago, a great American, in whose symbolic shadow we stand signed the Emancipation Proclamation. This momentous decree came as a great beacon of hope to millions of Negro slaves who had been seared in the flames of withering injustice. It came as a joyous daybreak to end the long night of captivity. But one hundred years later, we must face the tragic fact that the Negro is still not free. One hundred years later, the life of the Negro is still sadly crippled by the manacles of segregation and the chains of discrimination. One hundred years later, the Negro lives on a lonely island of poverty in the midst of a vast ocean of material prosperity. One hundred years later, the Negro is still languishing in the corners of American society and finds himself an exile in his own land.

Rev. Dr. Martin Luther King, Jr.

PREFACE

The Boiling Pot of Injustice clearly illustrates what can happen within a work environment when patterns of racial injustice are ignored by people in authority. Most importantly, when Christians choose to remain silent, they become the best kept secret in an atmosphere that reigns in the midst of darkness. When God created man and placed him in the garden, this was the beginning of this word called, "Sin;" however, because God is omniscient as well as omnipotent in scope, He knew that things would not remain perfect and there had to be another means that would require giving His son in order to rescue us from the terrible sins of damnation and the darkness of evil.

Sin has the tendency to spread like the sand upon the seashore. In the midst of these deadly evil's is the ugly and annoying sin of racism. Many teach and believe without doctrine or scientific support that certain ethnicities put superiority of one race over others and try with every fiber within their thinking to maintain this racial disharmony. Racism is systematic practically in every organization in the western world. In fact, it is often quoted that the most segregated hour during the week is at 11:00A.M. on Sunday morning.

Although we preach and teach that all men are created equal and endowed by God to be so, our actions are contrary and we do not put these words into practice when it comes to those who look, act, and live differently. This annoyance sin determines where we are born, live, work, and buried in the western world. Many of our religious and political leaders refuse to deal with this subject, because it cuts and hurts into the inner most fiber of our lives and it is easier to talk about the invisible soul, and let the body go hungry, cold, ill, and uncared for in this land of plenty.

Kelvin, it appears that you have unearthed the skeleton remains of racial discrimination and evil through your personal experience. Although these dry bones appear to be buried in a forgotten grave, this evil spirit has departed its resting place and embodied countless lives with the deep-seated illness that has contaminated this world. The sad reality of this topic will widen your eyes to the fear, cowardice and hatred when you witness the majority of the by standers will not follow or support you; nevertheless, this does not mean that you are wrong.

When Jesus wanted to clean up the lives of the Pharisees, Scribes, and Sadducees, the Jews resented Him for making them accountable for their actions. As a result, they refused to follow Him anymore and brought false accusations against Him in an effort to sentence Him in a kangaroo court to die. Although Pontius Pilot and others could not find anything wrong with Jesus, they still crucified Him.

Racism is like looking through dark glasses, we can never see the object clearly regardless of how much we may try to rationalize the evil and vicious deeds. Once more, the late Dr. Benjamin B. Mays encourages us to set goals and aim for them. "It must be borne in mind that the tragedy in life doesn't lie in not reaching our goal, but the tragedy lies in having no goal to reach." It isn't a calamity not to dream, but it is a disaster to have no ideal to capture. It is not a disgrace not to reach the stars, but it is a disgrace to have no stars to reach, so aim high my son and shoot for the stars.

Let me assure you in the words of the late Dr. Benjamin E. Mays, "He who starts behind in the race of life, must run faster or forever remain behind." Racism prevented us from having an equal and level playing field; therefore, we must run faster or therefore remain behind.

Rev. Dr. Simon Bodley, Jr.
Pensacola, Florida

PREFACE - II

One of the very painful facts about living in exile (both in biblical history and in African-American history) is the painful fact of assimilation and acculturation! Many exiles decide that the best way to deal with living in exile is to simply take on the culture of their oppressors! That is similar to following the least line of resistance.

Psychologists say that the thinking which produces that kind of assimilation reasons on this wise: If we can become like them then they will leave us alone! We won't stand out as much. That will cause them to back up off of us, not treat us so harshly and perhaps even make us "trusted exiles!"

In an often overlooked detail from the story of the three Hebrew boys thrown into the fiery furnace, the same principle can be seen. Likewise, in the story of Daniel's refusing to go along with a governmental mandate which prevented him from praying (as a matter of homeland security) the same principle is also demonstrated while overlooked!

As much as Bible readers' hearts are inspired by the stories of the three Hebrew boys who refused to bow and the story of Daniel who likewise refused to "go along to get along," the detail that is missed is what Kelvin Bodley writes about in this volume. The majority of persons who lived in exile went along with the government's game plan.

The majority assimilated. The majority acculturated. The majority did not stand up for what they believed in or what they had been taught to believe in their native land.

We often look at the courage, the faith and the determination of Shadrach Meshach and Abednego. What we miss, however, is that the other captives (the majority), the other persons living in exile and the other persons under oppression went along with the government. The same is true when it came to the matter of the governmental policies which prevented and prohibited praying!

Daniel stood his ground, but the majority went along with the government. That is what Kelvin Bodley ran into when he dared to challenge the governmental policies which are discriminatory and outright racist! He learned the biblical lesson the hard way.

Most of his own African-American brothers and sisters would not stand with him. Most of them were just like the "leaders" that Sterling Brown described in his poem "The Strong Men Keep Coming." Mr. Brown writes:

"They bought off some of your leaders
You stumbled as blind men will."

We know that some persons of African descent who live in exile in this "strange land" hold fast to the principles that their parents and fore parents instilled within them. Others, however, "go along to get along." Others "don't make waves." Others side with the government because they believe that the road of assimilation is a much easier road to travel than the road to liberation!

Just as there were Hebrews who could "out Babylonian the Babylonians," there are African Americans who have learned how to "out white, white folks!" That painful reality is what caused Mr. Bodley to examine his soul, examine his surroundings and write the very passionate piece that you now hold in your hands.

I ask you to read it through the lenses of the exiles who refuse to bow. Read it through the lenses of those who refuse to accept the definition as to who they are that is given to them by their captors.

Learn the lessons that Mr. Bodley learned. Pass them on to your children and your children's children and remember that whose you are (as the reality that is given to you by your Creator) is far more important than who or what the oppressor says that you are!

Pastor Jeremiah A. Wright, Jr.
Trinity United Church of Christ
Chicago, Illinois

PREFACE - III

The Boiling Pot of injustice is a must read book which illustrates how racial discrimination continues to burden people of color despite the numerous strides made as a result of the civil rights movement. The book begins to shine the spot light on people in authority who refuse to acknowledge that discriminatory practices exist in many of our private and government institutions in the 21st century.

The sad irony is the Boiling Pot of Injustice is symbolic of what can happen to innocent people when the reckless patterns of discrimination practices boils over into an institution and goes unattended as a result of fear and cowardice. A book such as this courageously takes the lid off and exposes the aroma of hatred and discrimination to those who wish to ignore the problem.

I also felt the harsh impact that discrimination can cause on the personal lives and professional careers of a person as outlined in Kelvin's book. The Boiling Pot of Injustice re-opened the wounds of training my white counterparts, who eventually were promoted to become my supervisor. As a result, I was forced to swallow the bitter pill of making less pay and doing more work in comparison. Furthermore, I was awakened to the cruel realism of being labeled with false accusations within a hostile work environment by my white counterpart's, where their word was unquestionably taken over mine despite the facts of the case. Unfortunately, throughout the years I have dealt with many of the same issues that the author of this book has suffered as an African American.

Kelvin in an eloquently manner writes about the subject matter of discrimination for us to recognize the problem will continue to burn innocent people if it's continually ignored. Therefore, I must commend Kelvin for taking the initiative to step out on faith and walk through the valley of the shadow of employment discrimination. Kelvin is right on track with the message of seeking equality for all qualified people regardless of race, gender or creed.

Thanks to books such as "The Boiling Pot of Injustice" the wanton patterns of racial discrimination are brought to the fore front so that we can recognize that there is still a lot of work ahead as we seek an equal playing field. This book does not just epitomize the trials and tribulation of one man against an unjust system, but represents the daily struggles as a race of people. Therefore, we must take up the mantel of fairness and justice and use it to fight for equality; however, we must never lose site of the prize, and understand by freeing our minds and spirits, that with God's grace, all things are possible.

Dwight N. Randolph
Orlando, Florida

**Kelvin shows appreciation for his parents,
Rev. Dr. Simon Bodley, Jr. & Mrs. Jenny Bodley**

DEDICATION

In dedication to my mom and dad Rev. Dr. Simon Bodley, Jr. and Mrs. Jenny Bodley who have taught me the importance of standing on the principles of having faith and trust in the Lord. Their words of support and encouragement have served as a beacon of hope as the Lord walked with me across the bridge over troubled waters. The countless lessons and discussions with my parents late in the midnight hour have been embedded within the archives of my soul and will forever serve as a reference guide for me to follow henceforth and forever more. God has blessed me along with my brother and sisters with a mom and dad that have understood the importance of assuming their rightful place as overseers to the predestination of God's promise. Words would not be enough to describe my appreciation for all that you have done for me throughout my short years of existence. The Prophet Isaiah said in Isaiah 11: 1 & 2, (KJV), *And there shall come forth a rod out of the stem of Jesse, and a Branch shall grow out of his roots: And the spirit of the Lord shall rest upon him, the spirit of wisdom and understanding, the spirit of counsel and might, the spirit of knowledge and of the fear of the Lord.*

DEDICATION

In dedication to the saints who jeopardized their professional careers by demonstrating their support on my behalf while I pursued a lawsuit against county government for employment & racial discrimination and retaliation. Mere words cannot express my heartfelt appreciation for witnessing my brothers and sisters in Christ stand on the principles of faith and truth in the midst of the storm. My prayers will forever remain with those saints whose names are not listed below and currently work with county government. The Prophet Isaiah said in Isaiah 43: 2 & 10, (KJV), *When thou passest through the waters, I will be with thee; and through the rivers, they shall not over-flow thee: when thou walkest through the fire, thou shalt not be burned; neither shall the flame kindle upon thee. Ye are my witnesses, saith the Lord, and my servant whom I have chosen: that ye may know and believe me, and understand that I am he: before me there was no God formed, neither shall there be after me.*

ROLL CALL

Laura Velez

Harland Bradley

Vivian Baker

Thomas McCarthy

**Bishop Woody E. Freeman & Elder Ella M. Freeman,
Full Deliverance Church of Jesus
and Rev. Dr. Willie C. Barnes, Macedonia Missionary
Baptist Church provided spiritual council to Kelvin D.
Bodley during his journey of discrimination.**

DEDICATION TO THE MINISTERS OF THE GOSPEL, LOCAL GOVERNMENTAL OFFICIALS, FAMILY & FRIENDS

It is with my sincerest heartfelt appreciation that I set aside this page to show my gratitude for the ministers of the gospel, local governmental officials, family and friends who looked beyond themselves to walk along my side through the valley of the shadow of employment discrimination. There continuous prayers of support, words of wisdom and guidance gave me comfort in the midst of the storm. The Psalm writer said in Psalm 91: 1-5,11, (KJV), *He that dwells in the secret place of the Most High shall abide under the shadow of the Almighty. I will say of the Lord, He is my refuge and my fortress: my God; in Him will I trust. Surely He shall deliver* you from the snare of the fowler, and from the noisome pestilence. He shall cover you with His feathers and under His wings shall you trust: His truth shall be your shield and buckler. You shall not be afraid for the terror by night; nor for the arrow that flies by day; For He shall give His angels charge over you, to keep you in all your ways.

ROW CALL

Rev. Dr. Willie C. Barnes, Macedonia Missionary Baptist Church, Eatonville, FL.

Rev. Dr. Jeremiah A. Wright, Jr. Trinity United Church of Christ, Chicago, IL.

Bishop Woody & Elder Ella M. Freeman, Full Deliverance Church of Jesus, Orlando, FL.

Prophetess Alexis L. Freeman, Full Deliverance Church of Jesus, Orlando, FL.

Bishop Victor T. Curry, New Birth Baptist Church of Faith Int. Miami, FL.

Rev. Dr. Rudolph McKissick, Jr. , Bethel Baptist Institutional Church, Jacksonville, FL.

Rev. Randolph & Dr. Lavon Bracy, New Covenant Baptist Church of Orlando, FL.

Rev. Dr. Earl B. Mason, Sr. Th.D. Bible Base Temple Terrace, Tampa, FL.

Rev. Dr. Arthur Jones, Bible Base Fellowship, Tampa, FL.

Pastor Abner Adorno, Living Word Church, Orlando, FL.

Rev. Christopher & Shakina Bodley, Our Savior Lutheran Church, Orlando, FL.

Rev. Dr. Simon & Jenny Bodley, Jr. Pensacola, FL. (Retired)

Rev. Arthur & Barbara Bodley, Pensacola, FL. (Retired)

Rev. Raymond Brinson & Men's Sunday School Class, Macedonia Missionary Baptist Church, Eatonville, FL.

African American Council of Christian Clergy, Orlando, FL.

Attorney Gary A. Siplin, Senator, 19th District, The Florida Senate, Orlando, FL.

Bruce Antone, State Representative, District 39, Orlando, FL.

Former Vice-Mayor Alicia Reece, Cincinnati, Ohio

Steven Reece, Sr., President, Communiplex Services, Cincinnati, Ohio

Orange County Commissioner Teresa Jacobs, District 1, Orlando, FL.

The Boiling Pot of Injustice

Family (Dad, Mom, Chenita, Ashley, Lemoyne, Jackie & Gloria)

Central Florida Black Journalist, Orlando, FL.

Frank & Janice Mitchell, Heathrow, FL.

Byron Brooks & Rufus Brooks, Orlando FL.

Ronald & Ruth Woodfork, Chicago, IL.

Daniel R. Gunn, & Henry Smith, Chicago, IL.

Timothy Shuler, Orlando, FL.

Anthony Whitfield, & Tracey Jenkins, Chicago, IL.

Dwight Randolph, Orlando, FL.

Rev. Prentice Marsh, Chicago, IL.

Tina Wells, Orlando, FL.

Ann Freeman, Orlando FL.

Minister Juvais Harrington, Miami, FL.

Chris Norwood, Orlando, FL.

JoeAnn McClandon, Heathrow, FL.

Melinda Poole, Heathrow, FL.

Camille Reynolds Humphrey, Orlando, FL.

Derrick Bodley, Chicago, IL.

Attorney Wanzo Galloway, Orlando, FL.

Reece Family (Steven Sr., Barbara, Alicia, Steven Jr., Tiffany) Cincinnati, Ohio

Attorney Larry H. Colleton, P.A. Esquire, Orlando, FL.

Beverly Neal, State NAACP Office, Orlando FL.

Minister Shaun & Jacquelyn Muse, Orlando, FL.

Yvonne , Merc & Curtis Thompson, Chicago, IL.

**Left to right:
Lemoyne, Kelvin, Jacqueline, Gloria, Chenita,
Rev. Dr. Simon & Jenny Bodley**

INTRODUCTION

The Boiling Pot of Injustice: Wounded by Cowardice was written to address racial discrimination and retaliation within the workplace. As an African American Christian man, the results of my personal experience of filing a lawsuit against my employer were apparent. If I ever needed the Lord before, I sure did need him during that difficult journey. I felt compelled to retrace my steps and recount the painful discriminatory process in hopes of helping other Christians should they be forced to deal with such an encounter within the workplace.

This experience opened my eyes to the harsh realities of the price that I paid when I stood up for my spiritual principles and challenged a bureaucratic system that rules on the premise of "Absolute Power." This new awakening afforded me an opportunity to gauge the debts of my endurance as it related to my faith in God. Most people never realize the significance of their faith until they are tested with trials and tribulations.

Employment discrimination has a way of separating the sheep's from the goats and identifying your real friends. This shrewd process slowly eliminates people through attrition and clearly opens your eyes to how unpopular you can become within a twinkling of an eye. Unfortunately, employment discrimination leaves an odor of fear throughout the workplace and can quickly make you feel as though you were diagnosed with leprosy.

Despite the difficult journey, God had blessed me by cultivating true friendships with a few saints sent by God

Himself to encourage me, and to stand alongside me in the face of evil. Although their names were purposely omitted from my book to protect their jobs, I was truly humbled and will forever reflect on their faithfulness and belief in God as they jeopardized their professional careers and financial stability to stand up for what was right opposed to what was safe and popular. Their commitment and dedication constantly reassured me through the most challenging moments that God was with us even though we were greatly out numbered by the opposition.

I would encourage anyone before they ever decide to undertake on such a monumental task of fighting for their civil rights, to pray and ask God for direction. If God does affirm your decision to stand against spiritual wickedness in high places, pray that God gives you a supportive family that not only understands the importance of faith, but believes in the promises of prayer. I thank my parents for their unwavering faith in God and continuous prayers during a critical time when our cries for help to the people in authority went unanswered. Nevertheless, my parent's words of encouragement always inspired me when I felt like giving up and abandoning the struggle for justice and fairness. I am forever grateful for my three sisters, Chenita, Jacqueline and Gloria for constantly leaving prayers and words of encouragement on the answering machine.

The Boiling Pot of Injustice: Wounded by Cowardice was written to expose Christians to the harsh reality of fighting against an organized system inundated with racial discrimination and hatred. Unfortunately, this cruel realism can abruptly shatter marriages, disturb family structures, strain friendships, destroy reputations and ruin you financially. As a result, the Boiling Pot of Injustice: Wounded by Cowardice appeals towards Christians to understand the significance of being your brother's keeper by being supportive in addition to sharing words of encouragement.

The Boiling Pot of Injustice

One of my best friend's shared with me that one of the greatest misconceptions in the Body of Christ is the assumption that just because we are Christians, we won't endure storms that would challenge our heritage identity and put us in the face of the type of adversity that as African Americans our fore-fathers faced years ago while fighting so that we won't have endure such hardships. Although we as a culture would like to believe that the fight is over, everyday there are countless signs and endless moments to remind us that the fight has not ended. The unfortunate plight to us is when we can witness this fight on a sophisticated level go unnoticed until one person recognizes the stain of injustice and decides to stand up for what they believe is right.

There were many occasions when I observed church folk witness the atrocities we were experiencing in the workplace and they simply maintained their silence and walked on the other side of the office and left us to defend ourselves.

There were also church folk who would walk by quickly and whispered a scripture and immediately return back to the dark shadows of their hiding place. Regrettably, they failed to understand James when he wrote James 2: 14-17, (KJV), *What doth it profit, my brethren, though a man say he hath faith, and have not works? Can faith save him? If a brother or sister be naked and destitute of daily food, and one of you say unto them, depart in peace, be ye warned and filled; notwithstanding ye give them not those things which are needful to the body; what doth it profit? Even so faith, if it hath not works, is dead, being alone.*

Although my dear friends and I suffered many days of affliction by being harassed and retaliated against by those in authority, we continued to rely on our faith in God, He promised never to leave us or forsake us. Most importantly, despite the difficult obstacles that were before us, we understood that everyday new mercies we saw through God's bountiful grace.

My purpose is to encourage Christians to allow their light to shine as they walk through their valley of shadow of employment discrimination. I attempt to deliver insight and advice from personal experience that one would only imagine enduring through this tumultuous journey and to open up the eyes of society to such quiet storms that are still lingering even in the 21st century. Although there is no guarantee the organized system will crumble like the walls of Jericho, there is an assurance that God will have the final say and that the truth will crest the earth. The Boiling Pot of Injustice: Wounded by Cowardice was written with an empathetic undertone that speaks volume to the one who feels alone in a similar situation. Therefore, the Boiling Pot of Injustice: Wounded by Cowardice warns those of us that if racial discrimination is allowed to simmer too long, hatred will eventually boil over and burn you.

The Apostle Paul wrote in the book of Ephesians 6:10-19, (KJV), *Finally, my brethren, be strong in the Lord, and in the power of his might. Put on the whole armor of God that ye may be able to stand against the wiles of the devil. For we wrestle not against flesh and blood, but against principalities, against powers, against the rulers of the darkness of this world, against spiritual wickedness in high places. Wherefore take unto you the whole armor of God that ye may be able to withstand in the evil day, and having done all, to stand. Stand therefore, having your loins girt about with truth, and having on the breastplate of righteousness; And your feet shod with the preparation of the gospel of peace; Above all, taking the shield of faith, wherewith ye shall be able to quench all the fiery darts of the wicked. And take the helmet of salvation, and the sword of the Spirit, which is the word of God: Praying always with all prayer and supplication in the Spirit, and watching thereunto with all perseverance and supplication for all saints; And for me, that utterance may be given unto me, that I may open my mouth boldly, to make known the mystery of the gospel, For which I am an ambassador in bonds: that therein I may speak boldly, as I ought to speak.*

Left to right: Kelvin D. Bodley & Frank Mitchell participating in the 2000 march in Tallahassee Florida in protest to One Florida by Governor Jeb Bush.

Chapter One

Enslaved Freedom

Oh, freedom! Oh, freedom! Oh, freedom over me! And before I'd be a slave, I'll be buried in my grave, And go home to my Lord and be free. No more moaning, No more moaning, No more moaning over me! And before I'd be a slave, I'll be buried in my grave, And go home to my Lord and be free. There'll be singing, There'll be singing, There'll be singing over me! And before I'd be a slave, I'll be buried in my grave, And go home to my Lord and be free. There'll be shouting, There'll be shouting, There'll be shouting over me! And before I'd be a slave, I'll be buried in my grave, And go home to my Lord and be free. There'll be praying, There'll be praying, There'll be praying over me! And before I'd be a slave, I'll be buried in my grave, And go home to my Lord and be free. (Arranged by Paul Abels)

Paul Abels song of freedom showed the conviction and spiritual fortitude displayed by many of our forefathers who would rather die and be buried in a grave in their quest to reach freedom in heaven opposed to being bound in shackles on earth through slavery. Their tireless walk towards freedom caused countless families to moan, sing, shout and pray as another lifeless body was being laid to rest in a dark hole within the earth. Nevertheless, because of their strong and unwavering faith in the Lord, they knew He reached down and snatched their soul from the cold hands of death into a life of eternal freedom.

The Apostle Paul preached it this way in 1 Corinthians 15: 12-15, 55, (KJV), *Now if Christ be preached that he rose from the dead, how say some among you that there is no resurrection of the dead? But if there be no resurrection of the dead, then is Christ not risen: And if Christ be not risen, then is our preaching vain, and your faith is also vain. Yea and we are found false witnesses of God; because we have testified of God that he raised up Christ: whom he raised not up, if so be that the dead rise not. O Death, Where Is Thy Sting? O Grave. Where Is Thy Victory?*

The fight for freedom continues to be a blurry vision of shattered intentions for many of us who still walk through the valley of shadow of racism and discrimination in our daily lives. I often have to refer to the Webster's Dictionary of the English Language Unabridged to remind myself of the meaning of "Freedom". Webster's stated freedom is the state or quality of being free; exemption or liberation from the control of some other person or some arbitrary power; independence; a being able to act, move, use, etc. without hindrance or restraint.

When I was attending high school, I was required to study and pass an examination regarding the constitution of the United States as a prerequisite to graduation. The following words within the constitution always stood out in my mind: "We hold these truths to be self-evident, that all Men are created equal, that they are endowed by their Creator with certain unalienable rights, that among these are Life, Liberty, and the pursuit of happiness--That to secure these rights, governments are instituted among Men, deriving their just Powers from the consent of the governed, that whenever any

Form of Government becomes destructive of these Ends, it is the Right of the People to alter or to abolish it, and to institute new Government, laying its Foundation on such Principles, and organizing its Powers in such Form, as to them shall seem most likely to effect their Safety and Happiness".

Whenever any form of government becomes destructive of these Ends, it will foster a political platform built on the selfish principals of corruption, voracity, haughtiness, wealth and absolute power; thus, eroding the foundation of truth, honesty, justice, equality, and compassion for those less fortunate. Consequently, government has been stained by politicians who have chosen to be consumed with selfish motives creating an atmosphere of dishonesty. More over, others have made the decision to simply close their eyes and ignore the injustice while quickly forgetting their oath of office to uphold and protect the rights of the people they swore to serve. Luke said, *For a good tree brings not forth corrupt fruit; neither does a corrupt tree bring forth good fruit. For every tree is known by its own fruit. For of thorns men do not gather figs, nor of a thorn bush gather they grapes. A good man out of the good treasure of his heart brings forth that which is good; and an evil man out of the evil treasure of his heart brings forth that which is evil; for of the abundance of the heart his mouth speaks. Luke 6:43-45 (KJV).*

Whenever any Form of Government becomes destructive of these Ends, it enslaves the freedom granted that all men are created equal with certain unalienable rights. This illicit method of enslaved freedom led me to point towards the muddy foot prints that confirmed an overt prototype that only one African American at a time was permitted to work in the Chairman's elite County Administration office on the fifth floor in a position of upper management. The muddy foot prints also led to the discovering that only one African American at a time has been permitted to serve in the position as a Director within middle management. The ideology has been consistent since the inception of it's creation of the Chairman position and the Board of County Commissioners within county government. This haughty approach has been blatant and concealed behind the iron curtain of government where the "Good Old Boys" have imposed a lifelong mandate of business as usual.

Whenever any Form of Government becomes destructive of these Ends, it keeps minorities shackled to fewer promotional opportunities towards upper mobility than compared to their white counterparts. In an effort to confirm my suspicions that more white employees with high school diplomas on average are paid more than African American's and Hispanics with college degrees in the same job classification, I requested a county Public Records Request in August 31, 2004 for all of the county employees in the areas of ethnicity, gender, job classification, date of hire, salaries, pay grade, and educational credentials. However, the county conveniently did not require recording the educational credentials in the Human Resources Department for each division to conduct that official comparison analysis in this area.

As a result, I was forced to make an educated hypothesis and determined that it was a lot easier for the county to grand father uneducated white candidates through the county system and afford them the best opportunity possible to become well verse in their current area of expertise irregardless of their lack of educational credentials; consequently, if someone wanted to validate this hypothesis, they could simply ask countless African Americans and Hispanics who met the minimum educational criteria for certain positions they applied in most cases; yet, were not afforded the same great opportunity as their white counterparts, because they failed to meet the minimum experience required on the employment application.

Nevertheless, I decided to conduct a random sample analysis based on my personal experience when I worked in the County Code Enforcement Division. The analysis clearly confirmed that every white supervisor since the inception of the Code Enforcement Division, only possessed a high school diploma and was paid equal too or more than the two African American supervisors that possessed between the two of them, Bachelor of Science degrees, Master's in Public Administration, Fire and Building Department Certification and had experience in their field of employment. Therefore, it is my opinion these statistics can be confirmed throughout various divisions should county government be required to provide that "Top Secret" information which conveniently has not been available for public records to expose the truth of the matter.

Further more, in an effort to measure a true time line of progression for African American's and other minorities in comparison to their white counterparts in the areas of promotions and salaries, I recently submitted an additional Public Records request to the Human Resources Department to start at the beginning when the county formulated the Board of County Commissioners and elected the first chairperson named Linda Chapman leading up to it's current Mayor Richard Crotty. However, in order to measure the trend of upper mobility regarding minorities working within this county government, I focused my attention on the following positions: Assistant Managers, Managers, Deputy Directors, Directors, Directors on the County Administration level, Deputy County Administrators and County Administrators.

The key measuring indicator will be to track any employee through the system that ever held the above referenced positions from the date of hire, termination and or current status within the county. In my humble opinion, should the county government happen to locate this critical data from the depths of the ocean next to the treasure chest containing the educational credentials, it will either display a commitment towards equal employment opportunities for all employees regardless of race, gender, sex, ethnicity, and gender, or it will expose a pattern of exclusion, salary disparity, and overt racial discrimination practices that plague a system that was founded on the principles of justice and fairness by the people and for the people. Of course, I don't mean to stir up any dead bones that lay along side the boiling pot of injustice, but, "I'm just saying."

Whenever any Form of Government becomes destructive of these Ends, justice is auctioned off to the highest bidder and freedom begins serving its sentence on death row. However, despite freedom being given a death row sentenced for Afro-Americans and many minorities, James Weldon Johnson understood it better when he wrote the National Negro Hymn, entitled "Lift Every Voice And Sing". *Lift every voice and sing, till earth and heaven ring, Ring with the harmonies of liberty; Let our rejoicing rise, high as the listning skies, Let it resound loud as the rolling sea. Sing a song full of the faith that the dark past has taught us, Sing a song full of the hope that the present has brought us; Facing the rising sun of our new day begun,* **Let us march on till victory is won.**

**Left to right:
Kelvin D. Bodley, Vivian Baker, Laura Velez and Harland Bradley**

Chapter Two

Walking Gracefully Through The Valley Of The Shadow Of Employment Discrimination

—∞—

Many employees experience discrimination at some point in their professional careers and then find themselves in an awkward predicament when seeking solutions towards addressing the problem. In some instances, employees can arrange a meeting with their supervisor and have the matter resolved before it escalates into an undesirable situation. However, other situations require an employee to request an independent investigation from an agency within the organization in hopes of obtaining an objective resolution.

Unfortunately, many employees are left with making these critical decisions to defend their civil rights without the intervention of management. Although there are many businesses and organizations that really focus on the importance of fair and equal employment practices within the workplace; there are corporations that contaminate the employment environment by neglecting to preserve and protect the civil rights of the employees. Therefore, the employee can exercise their civil rights and file a discrimination complaint with the Equal Employment Opportunity Commission or the Human Relations Commission.

Once the employee makes the commitment to stand up against the organizations discriminatory practices, they must learn how to walk gracefully through the valley of the shadow of discrimination within the workplace and fear no evil. David wrote in the book of Psalm 37:23-24 (KJV), "the steps of a good man are ordered by the Lord, and He delights in his way. Though he falls, he shall not be utterly cast down; For the Lord upholds him with His hand."

My experiences of employment discrimination within the workplace have taught me the significance of conducting a personal assessment of myself prior to taking the first step towards the long arduous journey. As a result, I focused on five areas in my life that were vital towards my preparation to walk gracefully through the valley of the shadow of discrimination within the workplace and fear no evil.

First, I had to re-evaluate the importance of having faith in God and not leaning to my own understanding when trouble comes my way. The Hebrew writer said in Hebrews 11:6 (KJV), *"But without faith it is impossible to please him: for he that cometh to God must believe that he is, and that he is a rewarder of them that diligently seek him."* This bold walk of faith is not a journey that can be endured by personal might or strength, nor can it be seen with the natural eye; however, it is a spiritual walk that forces you to conduct a self examination of your faith and belief in God.

A walk of faith can be a lonely journey when you make the decision to stand and defend your civil rights in the workplace. Friends and co-workers can become scarce and oblivious to the surrounding issues of concern to avoid possible retaliation. The decision to stand made me feel isolated, as if on an island by myself. However, let's remember that the Apostle John was also on an island of Patmos when the Lord spoke to him and inspired him to write the book of

Revelation. The Apostle John said in Revelation 2:10 (KJV), *Fear none of those things, which thou shalt suffer: behold, the devil shall cast some of you into prison, that ye may be tried; and ye shall have tribulation ten days: be thou faithful unto death, and I will give thee a crown of life.*

This walk of faith is a journey that allowed me to surrender all and not put my hope and trust in man when obstacles arose. The song writers, Judson W. Van De Venter and Winfield S. Weeden wrote, "All to Jesus I surrender, All to Him I freely give, I will ever love and trust Him, in His presence daily live, I surrender all, All to Thee, my blessed Savior, I surrender all."

Secondly, I prayed that the Lord would grant me the courage to stand up for truth and justice and to speak boldly for those who could not stand for themselves. I understood that courage would be essential for maintaining spiritual fortitude when facing an employment environment that displayed evidence of corruption and collusion. Most people can't imagine how they would react if their livelihood was threatened and the reality of unemployment appeared to be eminent. Fear has a way of sounding the alarm; the realization that trouble is near and headed in their direction.

Employees working in a hostile environment have to accept the reality of examining their options in the event the organization wrongfully terminates them. Many times employees are naive to the retaliatory consequences they can face by an organization after filing charges of discrimination. As a result, the employee fails to make preparations in the event such a situation occurs. Moses wrote in the book of Deuteronomy 31:6 (KJV), *"Be strong and of a good courage, do not fear nor be afraid of them; for the Lord your God, He is the One who goes with you. He will not leave you nor forsake you."*

Third, in order to walk gracefully through the valley of the shadow of discrimination within the workplace and fear no evil, I understood the importance of having compassion. Once an employee surrenders to the pressures of discrimination in a hostile working environment, they can easily find themselves reacting angrily in an effort to defend their integrity. As a result, people focus on the negative reaction they observed from the employee without seeing what precipitated that particular response. As a result, the reputation of the employee can become tainted within the working environment. The Apostle Peter wrote in 1 Peter 3: 8-9 (KJV), *"Finally, all of you be of one mind, having compassion for one another; love as brothers, be tenderhearted, be courteous; not returning evil for evil or reviling for reviling, but on the contrary blessing, knowing that you were called to this, that you may inherit a blessing."*

Fourth, I maintained humility in the midst of fighting to preserve my civil rights within the workplace. Oftentimes employees can create the perception they are condescending and self-righteous while defending a position they believe is correct. Therefore, the employee's personal conviction can be misconstrued as being arrogant and accused of having the wrong motive for filing the complaint of discrimination against the organization. The Apostle Paul wrote in the book of 2 Timothy 2:25-26 (KJV), *"In humility correcting those who are in opposition, if God perhaps will grant them repentance, so that they may know the truth, and that they may come to their senses and escape the snare of the devil, having been taken captive by him to do his will."*

Fifth, the employee needs to sustain their joy as they walk through the valley of the shadow of discrimination when they encounter evil within the workplace. It's important to understand that God is in control regardless of the outcome. Unfortunately, many employees demonstrate a defeatist attitude in their demeanor. As a result, the organization can instigate more incidents that contribute to stress and eventually force the employee to resign in order to get relief from the hostile environment. James wrote in chapter 1:2-5 (KJV), *"My brethren, count it all joy when you fall into various trials, knowing that the testing of your faith produces patience. But let patience have its perfect work, that you may be perfect and complete, lacking nothing. If any of you lacks wisdom, let him ask God, who gives to all liberally and without reproach, and it will be given to him."*

Finally, if anyone decides to walk gracefully through the valley of the shadow of employment discrimination while encountering evil within the workplace, I encourage you to reflect on the importance of having faith, courage, compassion, humility, and joy in the Lord and He will see you through.

Rev. Dr. Jeremiah A. Wright, Jr, Senior Pastor, Trinity United Church of Christ, Chicago, IL. & Kelvin D. Bodley

Chapter Three

Rev. Dr. Jeremiah A. Wright, Jr. - "Wounded by Cowardice:" 04/02/00

—⚉—

When Pilate saw that he could prevail nothing, but that rather a tumult was made, he took water, and washed his hands before the multitude, saying, I am innocent of the blood of this just person: see you to it. Matthew 27:24 (KJV)

Looking at a series of biblical sermons "Wounded for our Transgressions," based on the premise that Jesus was wounded by many things other than the nails and the spear. A coward is a person who lacks the courage to face danger; a person who lacks the courage to face difficulty; a person who lacks the courage to face opposition, or a person who is easily intimidated.

This is not only the random house dictionary definition of a coward; it is also a classic description of Pontius Pilate. Pilate was a person who lacks the courage to face danger. John gives us more detail about the early morning interchange between the colonial governor and the King of Kings in John 19:12 (KJV) *And from then on Pilate sought to release Him: but the Jews cried out, saying, if you let this man go, you are not Caesar's friend: whosoever makes himself a king speaks against Caesar.*

As African Americans, we need to always remember when you read the word of God; you're not reading a fairy tale of Rodney King's fantasy, "where we can all just get along." Jesus people were people like you and I; they were under siege, they were a colonized people. John 19:12 (KJV) *And from then on Pilate sought to release Him: but the Jews cried out, saying, if you let this man go, you are not Caesar's friend: whosoever makes himself a king speaks against Caesar.* Remember what happen in West Africa in the nineteenth century, when Europeans took over other people's country? The French took over Senegal, Cote d'Ivoire and the Gabon. Why do you think those Africans speak French today?

The Germans took over the Cameroon's from 1884 to 1919 and the British and the French took over from 1919 to 1961. Why do you think the Cameroon's speak German, English and French? They were colonized, that's why Europeans took over other people's countries. The Portuguese took over Angola and Mozambique. When I was in elementary school, the maps on the wall in the classroom called them Portuguese West Africa, and Portuguese East Africa. Why do you think Angola and Mozambique can speak Portuguese? They were colonized, that's why Europeans took over other people's countries.

John 19:6. (KJV) states: *When the chief priests therefore and officers saw Him, they cried out, saying, crucify Him, crucify Him. Pilate says to them, take you Him, and crucify Him: for I find no fault in Him.* The British took over Nigeria, Ghana, and Sierra Leone. Why do think the Nigerians, Ghanaians and Creole speaks English, they were colonized. The Europeans took over other peoples countries in West Africa, East Africa and South Africa in the 19th century and the same thing happen in the North Africa and Palestine in the first century where this text originates. The text confirms Europeans took over Jesus people's country.

African Americans quickly forget the parallels between what they are reading in here and what they are living out there. You need to place the text in what the Germans call, sitz im Leben. If you read a text out of context and that's what a whole lot of us do, then all you got is a pretext. A pretext is a subterfuge that often distorts what the bible is actually saying. As a result, you have to keep the text in its proper context.

The Europeans colonized people, information, and education while taking over other people's countries and were clearly in charge of North East Africa. In Matthew 27 and John 19, early on in the series of sermons we look at Peter, a close friend of Jesus, who wounded Jesus by denying Him. This is the same Peter who said thou art the Christ, Son of the Living God. That was in response to Jesus asking His disciples, who do men say that I am? Who do people say that I am? Secondly, who do you say that I am? Do you remember that? Now, do you remember where they were when Jesus asked those questions in Matthew 16:13 (KJV) *When Jesus came into the coasts of Caesarea Philippi, he asked His disciples, saying, Whom do men say that I the Son of man am?*

The word of God said when Jesus came into the coasts of Caesarea... How at the southern slope of Mount Herman in Galilee, in North Africa, do you get a city named after Caesar, Caesarea and Philippi? Because Caesar Augustus, a European gave the city to Harriett the Great. These people not only took over somebody else's country, they're now going to give them what they stole from somebody else. For instance, It's like the Europeans that took over this country from the Seminole, Piqua's, Arapaho, Navajo, Placebo, Cheyenne and the Apache and turned it around by giving land grants to immigrants to help them get readjusted.

If you read the text in its proper context, you will discover that Caesar, a thief, gave some land away that wasn't his to give in the first place. Caesar gave the city to Harriett the Great and when Harriett's son Phillip became Tedrok, Phillip rebuilt and renamed the city after Caesar and himself. The Europeans are clearly in charge and have colonized Palestine and Pontius Pilate is the colonial governor. Now the interchange in Matthew 27 and John 19 is an interchange between a colonial governor and the King of Kings. Pilate had talked with Jesus in John 18 and he had found no fault with Him.

Pilate found no fault in Him and in John 19:6 (KJV) *When, the chief priests therefore and officers saw Him, they cried out, saying, Crucify Him, crucify Him. Pilate says to them, take you Him, and crucify Him: for I find no fault in Him.* In other words, Pilate said, you can take Him; I find no fault in Him. The church folk said to the colonial governor we have a law and according to the law, He must die. John 19:7 (KJV) *The Jews answered him, we have a law, and by our law He ought to die, because He made Himself the Son of God.* Since He claimed to be the Son of God, this had nothing to do with European law. But the governor was afraid to go against local custom because he didn't want to endanger the fragile relationship between the colonized and the colonizer's.

A coward is a person who lacks the courage to face danger. John 19:8, 10 (KJV) *When Pilate therefore heard that saying, he was the more afraid. Then says Pilate to Him, speak you not to me? Know you not that I have power to crucify you, and have power to release you?* Pilate went back inside and explained to Jesus the reality of colonial power and politics. Colonial power, European power, Roman power, "Rome do be in Europe".

Pilate's actions are similar to Italian power, mafia power. The folks outside have Pilate scared, but he comes inside and takes out his fear on Jesus. Why didn't he throw his weight around outside while he decided to sell wolf tickets inside? Because he is a coward, that's why... Do you know how much power I have said Pilate? Why is it that when we are mad at folk or upset with folk on the outside, that we come home on the inside and take out our anger, fear and frustration on the folk that have nothing to do with the thing that we are really upset about?

The boss kicks our butts at the office and we go home selling wolf tickets by jumping all over everybody in the house. We experience some racism on the job, streets or on the way home and instead of confronting what it is that is upsetting us, we come home and throw our weight around and let everyone know who the real boss is.

Pilate was a coward... When Jesus answered Pilate's sociological threat with a theology fact. John 19:12 (KJV) *And from then on Pilate sought to release Him: but the Jews cried out, saying, if you let this man go, you are not Caesar's friend: whosoever makes himself a king speaks against Caesar.* When Pilate heard these words, he was intimidated and all he could foresee was difficulty ahead should rumors reach Caesar at the royal palace in Rome with embellished reports that he failed to crucify Jesus.

A coward is a person who is easily intimidated, and lacks the courage to face difficulty. The Jews screamed for Jesus blood and were opposed to Pilate's honest assessment of Jesus character. In other words, the Jews were in opposition, but a coward is a person who lacks the courage to face opposition.

The primary text states in Matthew 27:24,27 (KJV) *When Pilate saw that he could prevail nothing, but that rather a tumult was made, he took water, and washed his hands before the multitude, saying, I am innocent of the blood of just person: see you to it. Then the soldiers of the governor took Jesus into the common hall, and gathered to Him the whole band of soldiers.* Pilate took the cowards ways out despite having the troops to assist him maintain crowd control while protecting Jesus.

They gathered a group around Jesus, a European colonized army numbered about 500 men. Pilate not only had the troops, but Pilate had the authority and the power. The Europeans are clearly in charge and Pilate reaffirmed that point when he told Jesus how much power he had; however, Pilate lacked the courage to face the difficulty or the opposition that intimidated him. As a result, Pilate took the coward's way out by taking some water and washing his hands before the crowd and saying that he was innocent of this righteous man's blood.

Many of us may not use water to wash our hands of a situation, but we will choose not to get involved. Like a true coward, Pilate flogged Jesus, and whipped Him with a multi thong whip. Why? "You just said He was righteous and that you found no fault in Him. In addition, you just said there was no case against Him and after having a little talk with Jesus that He was alright." However, Pilate chose to whip Him publicly to gain the support of the crowd in an effort to maintain his popularity.

A coward is not only a person who lacks the courage to face difficulty and opposition; a coward is a person who is easily intimidated and puts on a show for the folks he doesn't like just to gain their approval. Jesus was wounded by the cowardice of a colonial power that was in the first century, but guess what happens in the 21st century? Jesus is still wounded by the cowardice of Christian people. In the first century it was a colonial power, but in the 21st century, it's a Christian people.

Cowardice means that you won't stand up for what you know is right. For example, white privilege is wrong and white supremacy is wrong. The way the United States Government has directly supported black suffering is wrong. Furthermore, the hypocrisy of whites that have been helped by the government now have the audacity to sound self-righteous, saying blacks should help themselves that is wrong! Every white racist that is against affirmative action is wrong and every Uncle Tom and color coon who is against affirmative action is not only wrong, they are stupid!

In case you went to sleep in civic and history class, white folks did not get to where they are all on their own initiative and their can do attitude. Reverend Dr. Martin Luther King said these words thirty-two years ago and I quote. "At the very same time that America refused to give the freed Africans any land through the act of congress, our government was giving away millions of acres of land in the west and mid west.

Which meant that our government was willing to support it's white peasants from Europe with an economic floor; our government, the same racist government that has helped whites and pushed blacks down; our government, the white privilege government, our government has radically mistreated black people in the name of education, in the areas of agriculture and government subsidy. If your Christianity does not cause you to address that reality, then you got a religion that is so out of worldly focused, that it ain't doing nobody no earthly good."

Reverend Dr. Martin Luther King said thirty-two years ago that Christians should stand up when they see something wrong. Dr. King went on further to say not only did our government give white Europeans land, our government built land grant colleges with government money to teach Europeans how to farm; "Talk King"; not only that, our government provided technical support to further there expertise in farming; "Talk King"; not only that, our government provided low interest rates loans in order for Europeans to mechanized their farm. "Talk King".

Dr King links white privilege and government support directly to black suffering. Even Ray Charles and Stevie

Wonder can see that! Dr. King concludes, in the 1960's many of these Europeans were receiving millions of dollars in federal subsidies not to farm and they're the same people telling the black man that he ought to lift himself up by his own bootstraps. These are the enemies of affirmative action. Any Christian who sees that and who knows that and who won't stand up for that is a coward.

Cowardice means you won't stand up for what you know is right. Let me tell you something, you can get all the colored preachers you want to run downtown and lick up behind the colonial governor all day long, but I'm going to stand, even if I have to stand alone. The A.I.D.S. crisis is real, you can avoid it or you can deny it all you want too, but I'm going stand if I have to stand all by myself. Slavery in Africa, debt reduction in the Subs Saharan Africa and the mis-education of our African American young people may not be topics you want to hear in your tongue-talking tabernacle, but I'm going to stand even if no body else will stand with me.

Cowardice means you won't stand up for what you know is right. Jesus is still wounded by the cowardice of Christian people. Cowardice secondly means like Pilate, you take the easy way out and wash your hands of it and walk away from it. Answer me a few questions, how do you walk away from crack addicted babies? How do you walk away from sexual abuse and domestic violence? How do you walk away from the debt crippling and choking the life out of the unborn black children while the fat cats get fatter? How do you walk away from your own people being held slaves in the 21st century? Do you think Jews would walk away if Jews were being held slaves in modern day slavery? How do you walk away from an educational system that does not educate? How do you walk away from a criminal justice system that locks black men up for just being near crack cocaine, but lets white cops kill and walk free after firing forty one shots into a unarm black man, how do you walk away from that?

How do you walk away from a political system that blocks almost every black judicial appointee submitted by President Bill Clinton, how do you walk away? How do you walk away and let Jessie Helms and Strom Thurman continue to rule the day, how do you walk away? How do you walk away and allow a confederate flag fly over a Capital building, how do you walk away and allow Alabama governor proclaim April as Confederate History month? I'll tell you how you walk away; you take the easy way out. You wash your hands of it and say, yawl do what you got to do.

Jesus is wounded by the cowardice of Christian people. Cowardice means that you won't stand up for what you know is right? Matthew 27:18-19 (KJV) *For he knew that for envy they had delivered Him. When he was set down on the judgment seat, his wife sent to him, saying, Have you nothing to do with that just man: for I have suffered many things this day in a dream because of Him.* Pilate knew that the only reason they handed Jesus over to him was because they were jealous. Pilate knew that Jesus was innocent because his wife sent a note to him, which confirmed what he sensed in his spirit and what his wife seen in her dream. Nevertheless, Pilate would not stand up for what he knew was right and neither would many of us.

Cowardice means you won't stand up for what you know is right. Cowardice means you like Pilate, take the easy way out, wash your hands of it and walk away from it. But cowardice also means that you choose flight over fight. For example, you run from it, "flight;" you go into denial, "flight." You pretend it ain't none of your problem, "flight." Jesus is still wounded by Christian people who choose flight rather than stand and fight. We run from our responsibility to participate in the political process. We run from the reality that some of the elected officials we have do not have our best interest at heart.

The Boiling Pot of Injustice

However, we act shock when the Mayor's cronies are caught with their hands in the till. We run from the hard questions like how come our church members get traffic tickets and the mayor's preacher members don't get tickets? We run from the racism that shapes our society and try to act like the race problem has been solved. For example, we got Clarence Thomas, Michael Jordan, Oprah Winfrey, and Denzel Washington and speaking of Denzel, can we talk Oscar's for just a minute? Can we talk Hollywood for just a second? Yawl don't own not "nan" nickel of CBS and CBS ain't the color broadcasting system, that's the colonial broadcasting system. They can kick City of Angels off, just like they put it on the air. CBS own it and like Pilate, they say we got the power to keep Him or to crucify Him!

The first black man to win an Oscar was 27 years ago back in 1963 when Sidney Portier won in Lillie's of the Field. Come on this is America. Your missing this, they drag James Berg to death, a black man. They shot Amadou Diallo down like a dog, a black man. They rammed the plunger up Abner Louima, a black man; they took the title from Muhammad Ali, a black man; they killed Dr. Martin Luther King, a black man; they murdered Megar Evers, a black man; They framed the Scottsboro Boys, they lynched Emmit Till, a black man; they passed the Dred Scott decision, a black man; they hounded Marcus Garvey, a black man; they persecuted Paul Robinson, a black man; they defamed W.E. B. Dubois, a black man.

We run from the racism that shapes our society and act like the race problem has been solved long ago. William Julius Wilson said it was solved. Ronald Regan said the race problem was solved; President George W. Bush Sr. said the race problem was solved; Supreme Court Justice Clarence Thomas said the race problem was solved. We run from reality rather than fight to change that reality. Jesus is still wounded by Christian people who choose flight rather than stand and fight.

Let me tell you why I ain't going to run. Do you remember that song, we are soldiers in the army; we have to fight although we have to cry. Well a verse of that song said, my mother was a soldier, she had her hand on the gospel plow, one day she got old, she couldn't fight on anymore, she said, I'm going to stand here and fight on anyhow. Out of respect for our mothers and fathers, giving honor to our Grand mothers and Grand Fathers, I got to stand here and fight on anyhow.

Why, because this battle is not ours, it's mine said the Lord. Why, because no weapon formed against me shall prosper. Why, because I don't care what it looks like when you see me standing, I'm not standing all-alone, the Lord is with me. Why, because I'm not fighting my battle, I ain't fighting for me, I'm fighting for unborn generations of black children who should not have to go through, what we had to go through, I'm fighting in other words for God, and God never fails; that's why I'm not worried about failing, I may fail as an individual, but God never fails. You may fail, your friends may fail, but God never fails. If you stand up for God and fight on God's side, God never fails.

It's time to trade cowardice for Christian Courage.

Chapter Four

"Just There!"

And Methuselah lived an hundred eighty and seventy years, and begat Lamech: And Methuselah lived after he begat Lamech seven hundred eighty and two years, and begat sons and daughters: And all the days of Methuselah were nine hundred sixty and nine years: and he died. (Genesis 5:25- 27 KJV)

Although Methuselah lived a life of longevity at the rightful age of nine hundred sixty and nine years, the bible only references that he "lived and died." Sadly, Methuselah had no other acknowledgments of record that were accredited towards any significant accomplishments to making a contribution to the world during his life as the oldest man to ever live. Further more, the bible never talked about if Methuselah had established a reputation from his wisdom obtained by the experience of living nine hundred sixty and nine years from people seeking him out to solicit answers to their problems.

It is very difficult to imagine a man as one of the oldest to ever live upon this earth simply remembered for nothing more than just being there to live and die without leaving any significant accomplishments for others to learn from as a result of his wisdom and experience. In order to make this article practical, I would like to ask the readers two questions, what would life be like if you were just there? Other than the bill collectors, would any body ever notice you were missing should the good Lord call you home to glory?

In a world where employment discrimination has become a way of life for many minorities despite the Equal Employment Opportunity Commission laws in place to protect and preserve their civil rights, many minorities have simply abandoned any hope of ever being afforded an equal opportunity to be treated fairly and justly regardless of their educational credentials and experience. In 2005 minorities are still striving towards becoming the "First" for consideration in upper managerial positions in a predominately white environment despite vast credentials and expertise in their professional employment field.

An award-winning author, Jessie Carney Smith wrote the book entitled, "Black Firsts", which introduced and explained the significance of the more than 3,000 individuals and events that showed African American's had accomplished 2000 years of extraordinary achievements. Ms. Carney Smith stated, "We don't know that things can be done, that dreams can be fulfilled, that great accomplishments can be realized, until somebody takes that first step and shows the way."

Employment discrimination has often fostered an environment of fear and political consequences to those minorities who dared to be first towards challenging the injustices within their place of employment. As a result, many employees have transcended into a posture of being "Just There" to avoid controversy rather than jeopardize their professional careers by standing up for what is right regardless of the penalty.

Many of us have either witnessed or directly experienced employment discrimination on our jobs; however, this conscious decision not to get involved and ignore the wanton patterns of employment discrimination have merely perpetuated this evolving cycle.

Being "Just There" is a simple pretext for someone existing without a cause or purpose in life. Many people find excuses to avoid helping others and become selfish and self-centered while focusing their attention on themselves. It was our African American ancestors that taught us the significance of taking an entire village to raise a child. The same African American ancestors understood the importance of working together despite having families sold into slavery and denied their inalienable rights to freedom and equality. It was the same African American ancestors that gave their lives for us to have the right to vote and apply for better jobs and higher salaries. It was the same African American ancestors that because of their unselfishness afforded us an opportunity to ride in the front of the bus; eat at the front counter in a restaurant that was once segregated, and obtain a quality education.

The Apostle Paul wrote in the book of (Galatians 5: 13, 17, KJV), *"For, brethren, ye have been called unto liberty; only use not liberty for an occasion to the flesh, but by love serve one another. For the flesh lusteth against the Spirit, and the Spirit against the flesh: and these are contrary the one to the other: so that ye cannot do the things that ye would."*

Employment discrimination can be detrimental to a person's health and mental stability; particularly when an employee is experiencing discrimination and no one expresses an interest that they care to help them during their time of distress. Unfortunately, being "Just There" can cultivate an environment where the employee is often the one labeled the troublemaker and subsequently forced out of the system through an illegitimate termination.

Mordecai confirmed the importance of selflessness when he spoke to Esther in the book of (Esther 4:13-14 KJV), *"Then Mordecai commanded to answer Esther, think not with thyself that thou shalt escape in the king's house, more than all the Jews. For if thou altogether holdest thy peace at this time, then shall there enlargement and deliverance arise to the Jews from another place; but thou and thy father's house shall be destroyed: and who knoweth whether thou art come to the kingdom for such a time as this?"*

As Christians, we need to conduct a self-examination of our personal lives to determine our purpose in life when we encounter such obstacles as employment discrimination. More over, we need to listen to the voice of the Lord to determine how we can be used to help God's children in the time of need. Although we live in a world that breeds selfishness and power, we must learn as Christians that we have a spiritual responsibility to help and encourage those people who can't help themselves regardless of the consequences. Then you will better understand why the Lord enabled you to be in a situation for such a time as this.

Kelvin D. Bodley conducting conversations on two telephones in an effort to gain support to address his concerns regarding racial discrimination and retaliation

Chapter Five

You Have A Right To Remain SILENT In The Workplace

When I was growing up, I seldom missed my favorite police television shows such as Dragnet, Hawaii Five-O or Adam–12. Despite the constant police chases and action scenes that kept me captivated to the television screen, the storyline always ended up the same. A police officer reciting the famous "Miranda Rights" to the criminal, "You have the right to remain silent, anything you say can be used against you in the court of law, you have the right to have an attorney present now and during any future questioning, if you cannot afford an attorney, one will be appointed to you free of charge."

Similarly, on our jobs many of us have observed action scenes that occur in the areas of sexual harassment, age discrimination, disabilities discrimination, racial discrimination, hostile working environment and salary disparity; yet, most of us have chosen to exercise our "Employee Miranda Rights" in order to avoid jeopardizing our professional careers. Therefore, if you rather not unearth those dead bones hidden in the corner of your closet or buried in the darkest part of your soul, I recommend that you respectfully remain silent while I walk you through the crime scene in my professional career with County Government.

As I escort you through this political crime scene you are asked to conduct a self examination and determine how many times you have exercised your right to remain silent in hopes of preserving your career status? However, let it be known that the right to remain silent perpetuates a continuous pattern of injustice by those who fear no consequences for their wanton actions on the vulnerable employees in the workplace.

Scenario -1

The County Chairman (Hispanic Male) issued an April 10, 2000 memorandum to the Board of County Commissioners terminating the County Fire Chief (White Male) for not meeting the needs and expectations of the community. Although the County Fire Chief (White Male) was terminated effective June 30, 2000, he was afforded the opportunity to stay in the position as interim Fire Chief at $105,123.00 per year until January 2001. Moreover, the County eventually created a new position for the ousted County Fire Chief as County Director of Capital Improvement Projects at an annual salary of $106,000.00. Despite the common knowledge of the Fire Chiefs discriminatory practices, his actions were inevitably rewarded by the "Good Old Boy System" and silence prevailed.

Scenario-2

The Animal Services Division Manager position has been vacant since 2000; however, when a highly qualified African American, Assistant Manager, County Parks & Recreation Department applied for the Animal Services Manager position in 2003, the County Administrator (Asian/Pacific Islander) informed the African American that even though he was qualified for the position, the County Administrator could not hire him because of sexual harassment allegations that were made by an employee in 1998.

Although the County's Office of Professional Standards conducted an investigation regarding the sexual harassment allegations and determined the complaint was not valid and the charges were unsubstantiated by the County Office of Professional Standards, the African American was still not afforded an opportunity to be considered for the Animal Service Manager position which currently is still vacant to date. Further more, the County Administrator stated at the time of my deposition, the complainant's mother threatened that she would go to the news stations if the County hired the qualified African American. As a result, the County Administrator indicated it was his job to protect the integrity of the County; therefore, he could not hire the African American for that position under those circumstances.

On the other hand, a white male working in the County Fire Department as Interim Manager, was accused of sexual harassment and the findings were validated. Rather than take disciplinary action, he was transferred to the Building Department to rectify the problem. In addition, the white male was later accused of sexual harassment charges again in the Building Department and was suspended for two weeks by the County. However, the white male was permitted to still work in the Building Department and later promoted to Interim Director of Growth Management & Environmental Services Department. However, the white Interim Director eventually retired years later while the County Administrator and Deputy County Administrator (White Male) joined him at the Administration Building to help celebrate his farewell party. Consequently, the retired white Interim Director currently is working as a consultant at the County's Convention Center. Despite this common knowledge of racial bias and lack of disciplinary action, his actions were also rewarded by the "Good Old Boy System" and silence prevailed.

Scenario - 3

An African American was hired as a Code Enforcement Inspector in 2003 and terminated for allegations that he falsified his employment application regarding his work history by the Manager (White male) of the Code Enforcement Division. Whereas, a (White/Hispanic) Senior Code Enforcement Inspector, falsified his employment application on two occasions by stating that he had an Associate Degree in Criminal Justice and a Business Administration Degree; however, in the course of my deposition the County became aware that the Senior Code Enforcement Officer did not obtain either degree and is still currently employed in the County Code Enforcement Division. Despite this common knowledge of racial bias and lack of disciplinary action, his actions were also rewarded by the "Good Old Boy System" and silence once again prevailed.

Scenario – 4

It is my opinion and personal experience when the county was unsuccessful in their efforts to force me to resign as a result of their continuous tactics of harassment and retaliation towards me in the workplace, the county conspired with management and eliminated my section by transferring my staff to the outer most parts of the world. For instance, although my section was identified as a model customer service section by upper management and recommended to assist with training and writing a customer service guide manual for the new call center, my section conveniently was labeled obsolete due to the advancements with an automation system.

As a result, my section was discontinued and my staff was transferred to the call center and I along with another staff member was transferred to Neighborhood Services, where I no longer had supervisory status and my duties would consist of answering the telephones and mailing out notices to the citizens informing them of community meetings. However, since one of my staff members conspired to file a complaint against me and the other staff member refused to confirm my allegations of racial discrimination and retaliation against the county, they were permitted to remain working in the Code Enforcement Division.

In theory the corrupt tactics made perfect sense; however, in their haste and excitement to exile me to the island of Patmos by any means necessary, they forgot to hide the trace evidence which displayed their vicious actions of hatred by merely reassigning my duties to a white Code Enforcement Officer, who had no supervisory experience and was clearly working outside of her job classification since she was originally hired to perform code enforcement inspections in the field. Once management notified the Chairman's office and the Board of County Commissioners to direct all complaints to the new contact personnel within the Division even though my section's duties were considered obsolete and no longer needed, the coast was clear to resume business as usual.

Although it is your privilege to exercise your right to remain silent in the workplace, where would we be if our forefathers remained silent and ignored the urgency of the struggle for freedom and equal rights for all people regardless of race, gender or creed?

If silence had prevailed, would the Voting Rights Act of 1965 be in existence?

If silence had prevailed, would restaurant owners be required to remove the "White Only" signs from their windows?

If silence had prevailed, would school classrooms be desegregated?

If silence had prevailed, would there be any black CEO's in fortune 500 companies?

If silence had prevailed, would you be living the life that you are today?

If silence had prevailed, would you have heard the good news of salvation through Jesus Christ?

Many of us continue to surrender our integrity to a blind eye of injustice in hopes of protecting our jobs without considering the long-term consequences our silence has on others in the workplace. As Christians, we have a spiritual responsibility to look beyond ourselves and not put our hope in man, but trust that God will put his hedge of protection around us as we stand for the righteousness in the workplace. The Psalm writer wrote in chapter 50, vs. 3 and 21 (KJV); *"Our God shall come, and shall not keep silence: a fire shall devour before him, and it shall be very tempestuous round about him. These things hast thou done, and I kept silence; thou thoughtest that I was altogether such a one as thyself: but I will reprove thee, and set them in order before thine eyes."*

You have a right to remain silent in the workplace or a right to create positive change through a voice of boldness and Godly wisdom.

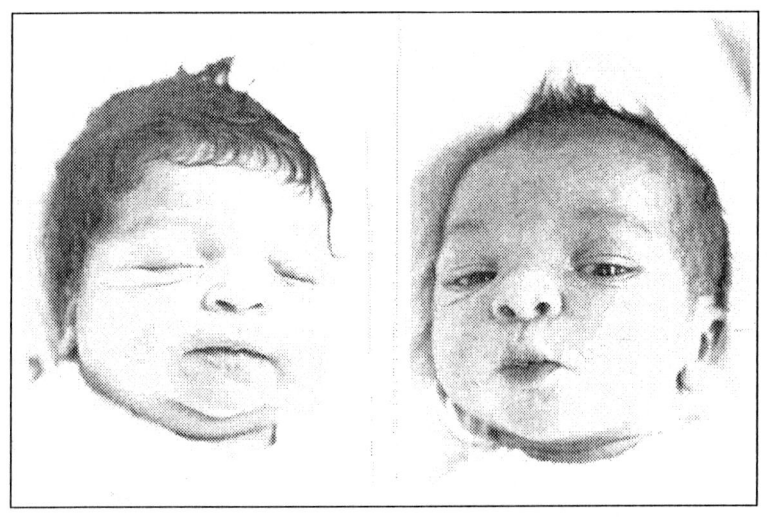

Kelvin D. Bodley opened his eyes once he heard the voice of the Lord call his name in preparation for such a time as this.

Chapter Six

Hush, Somebody's Calling My Name

And it came to pass, that, as I made my journey, and was come nigh unto Damascus about noon, suddenly there shone from heaven a great light round about me. And I fell unto the ground, and heard a voice saying unto me, Saul, Saul, why persecutest thou me? And I answered, Who art thou, Lord? And he said unto me, I am Jesus of Nazareth, whom thou persecutest. And they that were with me saw indeed the light, and were afraid; but they heard not the voice of him that spake to me. And I said, what shall I do, Lord? And the Lord said unto me, Arise, and go into Damascus; and there it shall be told thee of all things which are appointed for thee to do. (Acts 22: 6-10, KJV)

The question that I want to raise, which voice have you been listening to lately on your job? We live in a world that has been consumed with power, greed and disdain for our fellowman. Living in this midst it can be very difficult to ascertain which voice is speaking directly to you, particularly when it appears everyone is screaming at you and other co-workers at the same time in hopes of getting their urgent concerns and deadlines addressed.

Many times we try to avoid the never-ending stress of a hectic workday by blocking out everything around us in an effort to seek a few moments of solitude and avoid having a nervous breakdown. Ultimately, many of us slowly disappear into seclusion and simply focus on ourselves, becoming numb to our surroundings and refusing to feel the pain of fellow co-workers who are experiencing employment discrimination and possibly facing irreversible damage to their professional careers.

Matthew wrote in chapter 3: 1-3 (KJV), *In those days came John the Baptist, preaching in the wilderness of Judaea, and say, repent ye: for the kingdom of heaven is at hand. For this is he that was spoken of by the prophet Esaias, saying, The voice of one crying in the wilderness, prepare ye the way of the Lord, make his paths straight.* When was the last time you heard a voice from the wilderness call your name and yet you ignored it to avoid the guilt and shame of your participation in the persecution of co-workers through your direct or indirect involvement in employment discrimination? Luke stated in Acts 22: 20 (KJV) *And when the blood of thy martyr Stephen was shed, I also was standing by, and consenting unto his death, and kept the raiment of them that slew him.* Maybe you simply held your supervisors coats and merely watched while they harassed or retaliated against co-workers unjustly to assure they were terminated or forced to resign from the company.

The song writers Daniel March and J.C. Lenderman wrote, "Hark! The voice of Jesus calling, who will go and work today? Fields are white, the harvest waiting, who will bear the sheaves away? Loud and long the Master calleth, Rich reward He offers free; who will answer, gladly saying, Here am I, send me, send me."

It is difficult to discern the voice of the Lord when you're going through employment discrimination and you are out of fellowship with Him! There are times due to the enormous pressures and obstacles that are put in our way as a result of retaliation and discrimination in the workplace, that we often find ourselves looking for solace and affirmation through personal relationships and forget the significance of seeking fellowship with the Lord who can deliver us from evil. Despite all of the wise counsel we receive to help us through our journey of despair; ultimately, we will be left with making the final decision that will shape our lives forever regardless of the choice. David said in Psalms 119: 18 (KJV), *"Open thou mine eyes, that I may behold wondrous things out of thy law."*

How many times have we been told by friends, family or co-workers the unforgettable words of wisdom, "You can't help anyone until you first help yourself?" Theoretically the cliché makes perfect sense when you reflect on the significance of its meaning to put yourself first to avoid compromising your personal well-being at the cost of helping someone else experiencing employment discrimination; however, the meaning of this cliché takes on an entirely new definition if you're the one on the receiving end needing the help. The Apostle John wrote in the Third Epistle of John: 3-8 (KJV), *"For I rejoiced greatly, when the brethren came and testified of the truth that is in thee, even as thou walkest in the truth. I have no greater joy than to hear that my children walk in truth. Beloved, thou doest faithfully whatsoever thou doest to the brethren, and to strangers; which have borne witness of thy charity before the church: whom if thou bring forward on their journey after a godly sort, thou shalt do well: Because that for his name's sake they went forth, taking nothing of the Gentiles. We therefore ought to receive such, that we might be fellow helpers to the truth."*

Every one of us will eventually have a Damascus experience and hear a voice from the wilderness call our name as we stumble upon a problem in the workplace. It has been my personal experience as I encountered employment discrimination on my Damascus trail within the workplace, many of the "Church Folk" chose to remain silent and looked the other way in hopes of avoiding a direct collision with injustice.

Unfortunately, as I attempted to abstract evidence in search of the truth, it was many of the "Church Folk" that served as eyewitnesses to the wrongdoing that experienced "Spiritual Amnesia" as they whispered softly the unforgettable words, "I Don't Recall." It was many of the "Church Folk" that made the decision to submit false sworn statements to the opposing counsel in hopes of saving themselves. It was many of the "Church Folk" who helped perpetuate the rumor that I was obsessed with the lawsuit and determined to ruin fellow co-workers professional careers by jeopardizing their tremendous strides which took many years to progress from the "Field" to the "Back Porch." But I also had to come to the realization that everybody talking about heaven ain't going. Let the Church say, "Amen."

Yet through it all, there were a few "Christian Folk" who maintained the faith and provided words of encouragement at a time when I needed it most. It was a few "Christian Folk" who firmly believed the Lord had put them there to help me for such a time as this. It was a few "Christian Folk" who exercised their faith and works to assure that I obtained information to substantiate my allegations. It was a few "Christian Folk" that put their professional careers on the line to stand up for what they believed by being their brother's keeper. It was a few "Christian Folk" that inspired me through scriptures and song to maintain the faith and know that the Lord would never leave me nor forsake me. Despite the rough journey of experiencing employment discrimination, it was a few "Christian Folk" that reminded me when I complained about my troubles, "Hush, Somebody's Calling My Name."

Kelvin D. Bodley graduated in 1998 from University of Central Florida with a Masters Degree in Public Administration

Chapter Seven

"To Be Or Not To Be, That Is The Question?"

The Apostle Paul wrote in 2 Timothy 1:5-8, & 11-13,(KJV), *When I call to remembrance the unfeigned faith that is in thee, which dwelt first in thy grandmother Lois, and thy mother Eunice; and I am persuaded that in thee also. Wherefore I put thee in remembrance that thou stir up the gift of God, which is in thee by the putting on of my hands. For God hath not given us the spirit of fear; but of power, and of love, and of a sound mind. Be not thou therefore ashamed of the testimony of our Lord, nor of me his prisoner: but be thou partaker of the afflictions of the gospel according to the power of God. Whereunto I am appointed a preacher, and an apostle, and a teacher of the Gentiles. For the which cause I also suffer these things: nevertheless I am not ashamed: for I know whom I have believed, and am persuaded that he is able to keep that which I have committed unto him against that day. Hold fast the form of sound words, which thou hast heard of me, in faith and love which is in Christ Jesus.*

The Playwright William Shakespeare once said, "To Be or Not To Be, that is the question?" One day when we arrive at the cross roads of truth and injustice within the workplace, all of us will be forced to make the unavoidable decision of choosing to do what is spiritually right in the name of the Lord, or what is politically correct in the eyes of those that appear to have all power and authority over your professional career. The question will remain how your carnal or spiritual choice will affect those whose careers remain in the balance upon your decision.

I reflected on my colleagues that were subpoena during my deposition to affirm my allegations of racial discrimination and retaliation. Although I knew everyone fairly well and was aware of their knowledge regarding the facts of my case since they were eye witnesses to many of the wanton pattern's of racial discrimination and retaliation tactics perpetrated by county government towards myself, I knew they were going to be faced with making the ultimate decision of either testifying based on the truth and the facts of the case or pulling the rip cord of temporary amnesia.

History has proven that many people will simply continue to ignore the cruel realities of racial injustice until their professional careers and personal livelihood are threatened. Nevertheless, everyone is going to be faced with reaching the inevitable crossroads in their professional careers and making a critical decision to either stand up to address the wrongs or seek cover from the injustices to avoid any possible conflict. This personal conviction is a decision that will require courage and faith in the Lord prior to choosing between our carnality and spirituality. Often times many of us underestimate the grave price that will be required of you to stand up for what is right in the eyes of evil, opposed to remaining silent to avoid retribution and preserve one's personal or professional status. Moses wrote in Deuteronomy 11: 26-28 (KJV) *Behold, I set before you this day a blessing and a curse; a blessing, if you obey the commandments of the Lord your God which I command you this day: and a curse, if you will not obey the commandments of the Lord your God, but turn aside out of the way which I command you this day, to go after other gods, which you have not known.*

It was my belief during the time my legal council was conducting depositions with fellow co-workers, the county spared no expense to intimidate the employees that were providing sworn statements at the time of their depositions. For instance, the county had decided to hand picked the only African American Director in the county to represent them and sit on all of the depositions to assure the employees knew without a reasonable doubt that anything they said would be duly noted and reported back to the "Big House." As a result, words could not express the feeling of fear and frustration that pierced through the depths of my soul, when the statements, "I Don't Recall" were reverberated repeatedly by many of my colleagues. Although my spirit was shattered with frustration, disbelief and sadness, I continued to rely on my faith in the Lord for restoration in hopes of avoiding being consumed with the bitter cup of betrayal and cowardice. However, it appeared as though a thick cloud of fear hovered over the table as the opposing legal council and their hand pick county "colored" representative sat there staring down the witnesses to give surety they followed their prepared script of silence.

However, I was reminded of James when he raised the question regarding bitterness and enviousness in James 3: 11-17 (KJV) *Does a fountain send forth at the same place sweet water and bitter? Can the fig tree, my brethren, bear olive berries? Either a vine, figs? So can no fountain both yield salt water and fresh? Who is a wise man and endued with knowledge among you? Let him show out of a good conversation his works with meekness of wisdom. But if you have bitter envying and strife in your hearts, glory not, and lie not against the truth. This wisdom descends not from above, but is earthly, sensual, and devilish. For where envying and strife is, there is confusion and every evil work.*

But the wisdom that is from above is first pure, then peaceable, gentle, and easy to be entreated, full of mercy and good fruits, without partiality, and without hypocrisy.

To be or not to be is the question many of us can only began to answer once we conduct an internal assessment and examine ourselves in the areas of spirituality, integrity and ethics. Consequently, no matter how good the person's intentions and heart may be when confronted with discrimination, their actions will ultimately unveil the true measure of their character. For example, the Tom Joyner Morning show referenced an article, November 21, 2005, written by Michael H. Cottman of Black AmericaWeb.com entitled, "Two Democratic NAACP Leaders in Florida Switch to Republican Party."

The article revealed in Orlando and St. Petersburg Florida how Republicans have pulled off a controversial political coup, when they convinced two prominent longtime black Democrats, Derrick Wallace, President of the Orange County NAACP and Darryl Rouson, a former President of the St. Petersburg NAACP to switch political parties. Being a resident of Orlando, Florida, I feel it's only fair to shine the spotlight on the decision of Mr. Wallace to come out from hiding in the closet to "publicly" announce his "private" politics. "To Be or Not To Be" that is the question when Mr. Wallace confessed with his mouth in the article when he stated that it was a business decision, considering that ninety percent of the clientele for his construction company are Republicans.

"To Be or Not To Be" that is the question those of us must answer when we evaluate Mr. Wallace's civil rights resume under his leadership as President of the Orange County NAACP Branch office.

"To Be or Not To Be" that is the question, when you began to interview the complainants that filed claims with Mr. Wallace, President of the Orange County NAACP

Branch office to determine if any action was ever taken on their behalf.

"To Be or Not To Be" that is the question, when you began to search through the legal docket for cases of discrimination filed on behalf of the complainants from Mr. Wallace, President of the Orange County NAACP Branch office.

"To Be or Not To Be" that is the question, when you began to rummage around in the archives for the last public press conference led by Mr. Wallace, President of the Orange County NAACP Branch office with an action plan against any injustice that plagued the community.

"To Be or Not To Be" that is the question, when you can review the Equal Employment Opportunity Report prepared by Mr. Wallace, President of the Orange County NAACP Branch office, to assess if African Americans are afforded their fair share of employment opportunities in the areas of job classification, educational credentials, experience, salaries and promotions in comparison to our white counter parts.

"To Be or Not To Be" that is the question, when you can review the fundraising report and determine how many programs were funded for scholarships, legal defense fund, youth & senior programs, community awareness, workshops, food banks, employment training and literacy programs under the watchful eye of Mr. Wallace as President of the Orange County NAACP Branch office.

"To Be or Not To Be" that is the question that can simply be answered through the "actions" or "inactions" of the honorable Mr. Wallace as President of the Orange County NAACP Branch office.

As I began to reflect on the significance of answering this critical question, "To Be or Not To Be," I had to refocus the spotlight on the County Chairman's Office, County Administrator's Office, Board of County Commissioners, Management and the Office of Professional Standards, when they became aware of the atrocities that were occurring within the Code Enforcement Division; yet no official investigation was ever conducted to address the serious allegations of racial discrimination and retaliation.

Even though I established professional relationships with each office as a result of supervising a section that addressed an average of 4500 complaints per month, I clearly understood that I was still an African American within a "Good Old Boy" system; even though the Citizen Coordination Section I supervised was used as a model for the new Call Center to emulate quality customer service throughout the county, I clearly understood that I was still an African American within a "Good Old Boy" system; even though my section received countless emails and certificates of acknowledgment for being responsive towards the needs of the citizens of Orange County, I clearly understood that I was still an African American within a "Good Old Boy" system; even though citizens sent letters of accolades to the Chairman's office for the quality customer service demonstrated by the Citizen Coordination Section, I clearly understood that I was still an African American within a "Good Old Boy" system; even though I was considered the official liaison for the Code Enforcement Division to correspond with the Chairman and the Board of County Commissioners office, I clearly understood that I was still an African American within a "Good Old Boy" system, who's issues were unimportant and not going to dictate an ounce of an investigation that would embarrass the elitist establishment. Therefore, the question, "To Be or Not To Be" was answered in their actions of silence and arrogance by ignoring my plea for justice and fairness.

As I began to reflect on the significance of answering this critical question, "To Be or Not To Be," I had to shift the spotlight on my appeal to the African American, Hispanic and White Churches, Black Journalist, Public Officials, Attorneys, Co-Workers, NAACP, Friends, Family and various community organizations, and thank the Lord for

The Boiling Pot of Injustice

those that gave ear to my concerns. Although the results of the case did not come out like I would have hoped for during the time of my struggle for justice and equality, I am forever grateful of the efforts and sacrifices made on behalf of those that stood by my side.

Therefore, as we use this journey to reflect on the work that must be done to correct the wrongs of discrimination, I leave my brothers and sisters in Christ with these departing words as I attempt to address this poignant question, "To Be or Not To Be."

If Jesus were in my position, could He have relied on your efforts to pronounce His innocence during this struggle of facing the gallows of racial discrimination and retaliation?

"Don't Answer That, I'm Merely Raising The Question"...

"For I know the thoughts that I think toward you, says the Lord, thoughts of peace, and not of evil, to give you an expected end. Then shall you call upon me, and you shall go and pray to me, and I will hearken to you."
Jeremiah 29:11-12 KJV

Chapter Eight

Fighting Employment Discrimination – Is the Lord on your side?

The Lord has led countless activists who had the courage to fight for civil rights to establish equal employment opportunities for everyone regardless of race, creed or gender. History will corroborate throughout the years many sacrifices were made and lives were lost as people died in their fight for freedom. Although great strides have been made through the struggle for justice and equality, many minorities are still facing the harsh reality of racial discrimination on their jobs. Evidence of minorities being separate and unequal from whites can easily be identified in corporations and agencies through the areas of inequitable salaries, educational credentials and upper managerial positions.

As the fight against employment discrimination continues, many minorities are forced to make difficult decisions regarding unfair employment practices on the job that effect their professional careers. The decision to expose employment discrimination on the job can often lead to retaliation if the organization refuses to acknowledge the problem exists. Moreover, if management is negligent towards protecting the civil rights of the employees, the employment environment can quickly become hostile and unbearable. In many instances, the conduct of an employee can contribute positively or negatively towards the health and safety of their co-workers and the working environment.

Although many co-workers choose to remain silent to avoid the possibility of retaliation, they ultimately stand to benefit from the actions of the complainant should they prevail in their efforts; however, the organization can become sensitive to criticism and may weigh the political consequences of admitting guilt by correcting the problem and risk exposing the organization's weaknesses. As a result, the organization may select to challenge the integrity of the employee and focus on possible methods to discredit them. Consequently, the employee has to make the tough decision to either endure possible criticism for standing on their principles, or surrender their integrity by ignoring the injustice within the organization.

Unfortunately, many employees fail to acquire good counsel after making the decision to file a complaint of discrimination within the workplace. As a result, they are unaware of the political and bureaucratic dynamics that could be detrimental to the process. The political and bureaucratic dynamics can either hinder the results of an investigation or induce a decision to eradicate the problem to avoid negative publicity within the organization. Therefore, many employees are discouraged and abstain from pursuing the complaint of discrimination and the issues never get resolved; however, Luke wrote in chapter 14: 28-30 (KJV), *"Suppose one of you wants to build a tower. Will he not first sit down and estimate the cost to see if he has enough money to complete it? For if he lays the foundation and is not able to finish it, everyone who sees it will ridicule him, saying, this fellow began to build and was not able to finish."*

The cruel reality of becoming an advocate for justice within the workplace can be a journey of loneliness and long-suffering. Everyone is not a supporter of change in the workplace especially those participants that are beneficiaries from the illicit practices. Consequently, the employee may have a difficult time gathering support to challenge the discriminatory practices within the agency. As a result, the employee is left with the dilemma of searching for direction and support from friends, family or co-workers. This experience can have people of faith doubting and questioning themselves whether the Lord has abandoned them while they face the difficult task of filing an employment discrimination grievance; however, David wrote in Psalm 121: 1-2 (KJV), *"I will lift up my eyes unto the hills from whence comes my help? My help comes from the Lord, who made heaven and earth."*

If an employee would like to assure the Lord is on their side when fighting employment discrimination within the workplace, they need to conduct a self-examination in the following three areas:

First, the employee needs to have a personal relationship with the Lord to understand the promises of Christ, which will enable them to accept His perfect will regardless of the outcome. This personal relationship will allow the employee to have peace in the midst of the trials and tribulations. By having that relationship with the Lord, the employee will be able to walk by faith and not react to trouble that could surround them on every side. The song writers H.G. Spafford and P.P. Bliss wrote the song entitled, "It is well with my soul," which states: "When peace, like a river, attendeth my way, when sorrows like sea billows roll; whatever my lot, thou hast taught me to say, it is well, it is well with my soul."

Furthermore, the employee will understand the importance of letting the Lord lead and guide them on this spiritual journey in order to fulfill the Lord's purpose and plan. Often times, employees become bitter when friends, family and co-workers fail to support them after they file the employment discrimination complaint. Nevertheless, the employee must focus on what is right and think about the consequences should they decide to do nothing. The Hebrew writer said in chapter 13:5-6 (KJV), *"Let your conduct be without covetousness, and be content with such things as you have. For He Himself has said, I will never leave you nor forsake you. So we may boldly say: The Lord is my helper; I will not fear. What can man do to me?"*

Secondly, the employees must be able to look beyond themselves and consider the ramifications of the employment discrimination and the welfare of others within the workplace. Understandably, this is a difficult decision when other co-workers display a selfish attitude towards supporting the employee's allegations of discrimination. Unfortunately, most employees choose not to get involved in controversial issues to avoid jeopardizing their future promotions or benefits from the organization. However, the Lord looks favorably on those who show love towards people even when they are treated harshly in exchange for their kindness. Most importantly, the Lord is on your side when you forgive those people who don't understand the harm they inflict upon others.

If someone has the courage to stand and raise the question, there is high probability that the work environment will be better for all employees. Regrettably, many would rather look the other way than deal with the discrimination in hopes of reaching retirement age unscathed. On the other hand, making the personal sacrifice of taking a stand against the employment discrimination may ultimately benefit not only those currently employed in the organization but also those that will follow. David confirmed God is a refuge of the righteous when he raised the question by writing Psalms 94:16-17 (KJV), *"Who will rise up for me against the evildoers? Who will stand up for me against the workers of iniquity? Unless the Lord had been my help, my soul would soon have settled in silence."*

Third, the employee must have a sound mind and not have a spirit of fear when facing trials as a result of employment discrimination. Incidents can arise where the employee is offered a compromise to address the immediate problem without correcting the issue of employment discrimination within the workplace. As a result, in the event the employee disagrees with the compromise agreement offered by management, there is a possibility the employee can encounter extreme opposition from co-workers as well as management disagreeing with there assessment that employment discrimination exists within the place of work.

Once organizations exercise their rights to challenge the charges of employment discrimination, employees can become ostracized and treated as though they are the problem. Unfortunately, many employees are forced to stand-alone regardless if the facts support their allegations. Therefore, the employee has to weigh the consequences of their decision to fight against discrimination regardless of the cost. The Apostle Paul wrote in 1Timothy 1:7 (KJV) *"For God hath not given us the spirit of fear, but of power, and of love, and of a sound mind."*

I would like to commend those employees who unselfishly found the courage to stand in the midst of controversy for the betterment of others by filing a complaint of employment discrimination. Although the journey for justice and truth is long and arduous in the absence of support, if people continue to close their eyes to the injustice within the workplace, there will always be a need to struggle for equality and fairness.

Chapter Nine

Thanks Lord, "I'll Take It From Here"!

My brethren, count it all joy when ye fall into divers temptations; knowing this, that the trying of your faith worketh patience. But let patience have her perfect work, that ye may be perfect and entire, wanting nothing. If any of you lack wisdom, let him ask of God, that giveth to all men liberally, and upbraideth not; and it shall be given him. But let him ask in faith, nothing wavering. For he that wavereth is like a wave of the sea driven with the wind and tossed. For let not that man think that he shall receive any thing of the Lord. A double minded man is unstable in all his ways. (James 1:2-8 KJV)

James, the brother of Jesus, a leader in the Jerusalem church, was a bondservant of God and of the Lord Jesus Christ. He took on the challenge of exposing hypocritical practices and to teach the correct Christian behavior. James was concerned that the early believers did not have the support of established Christian churches. As a result, James wrote to them as a concerned leader to encourage them in their faith during those difficult times.

Often times as Christians, many of us experience frustration and disappointment as we undertake challenges in the course of our professional careers. History has proven that our ancestors had endured racism and hatred solely because of their skin color. Unfortunately, the old cliché still rings true, "the more things change, the more they remain the same." Nevertheless, as Christians we must continue to hold fast to the promises of Christ. We must be opposed to allowing our emotions to dictate a careless course of retaliatory action towards our perpetrator.

There are some Christians who believe because they are the Lord's children; the Lord is going to immediately rain down fire and hail stones on their enemies as soon as they finish praying. Consequently, due to our impatience many of us already have our minds made up prior to praying, only to inform the Lord of our real intentions. As a result, we seek out friends and family to affirm our actions and show them how the Lord allegedly supports us by displaying scriptures without hearing a word from the Lord.

The Apostle Paul wrote 1 Thessalonians 5: 14-22 (KJV), *"Now we exhort you, brethren, warn them that are unruly, comfort the feebleminded, support the weak, be patient toward all men. See that none render evil for evil unto any man; but ever follow that which is good, both among yourselves, and to all men. Rejoice evermore. Pray without ceasing. In every thing give thanks: for this is the will of God in Christ Jesus concerning you. Quench not the Spirit. Despise not prophesying. Prove all things; hold fast that which is good. Abstain from all appearance of evil."*

Although Christians face adversities on the job, the true test we must face is demonstrated in our obedience to the Lord. So often we have a tendency to deal with our enemies in our own way, opposed to allowing the Lord to order our steps and provide us with the wisdom necessary to go through our excruciating journey. No matter how difficult the situation, Christians must never forget that the Lord is ultimately in control regardless of the outcome. Even in the late midnight hour, when we feel all alone and have given up all hope because things appear to have not gone our way, we need to remind ourselves the Lord is still on the throne and promised to never leave us nor forsake us regardless of our circumstance. I often reflect on the dreadful journey of our ancestors when I hear the deacons line the hymn written by William Williams and Thomas Hastings, entitled: Guide Me, O Thou Great Jehovah.

Despite the countless tribulations and hardship our ancestors often endured through slavery, I can still hear their outcry to the Lord as they sang Guide me, O Thou great Jehovah, Pilgrim thro' this barren land; I am weak, but Thou art mighty, Hold me with Thy powerful hand: Bread of Heaven, Feed me till I want no more; Bread of heaven, Feed me till I want no more. Open now the crystal fountain Whence the healing waters flow; Let the fiery, cloudy pillar Lead me all my journey thro': Strong Deliverer, Be Thou still my strength and Shield; Strong Deliverer, Be Thou still my Strength and Shield.

How many times have you interfered with the Lord's plans and forfeited your blessing by meddling in the process? The Lord's does not need a personal advisor? The bible provides a number of illustrations of what happens when we ignore the voice of the Lord and relies on our own volition.

Adam and Eve had to deal with the consequences, when they said, "Lord, I'll take it from here," and bit into the forbidden fruit with the hope of being like gods and knowing good and evil. As a result of their disobedience, we have been dying ever since they fell into temptation; Moses had to deal with the consequences, when he said, "Lord, I'll take it from here," when he became angry with the children of Israel and struck the rock for water and failed to acknowledge the Lord in the process. As a result of Moses momentary laps, he was prohibited from entering into the promise land with the children of Israel; the children of Israel had to deal with the consequences as a result of their rebelliousness and disobedience, when they said, "Lord, I'll take it from here," when they ignored Joshua and Caleb describing how the Lord had prepared the promise land for them and it was only a three day journey; however, their fear of the giants rapidly transformed a three day journey into forty years and only their children along with Joshua and Caleb were afforded the opportunity to enter the promise land.

James understood the significance of seeking wisdom and relying on the promises of the Lord and not taking matters into his own hands. It was essential for James to challenge the church and expose hypocritical practices and teach them the correct Christian behavior. Most importantly, it was imperative that James as a leader encouraged the church to walk by faith and not by sight.

As Christians we allow our emotions and tongue to get us in trouble by expressing ourselves to others in the heat of the moment. As a result, we undermine our spiritual walk as Christians and send the wrong message through our actions as witnesses for the Lord; however, James warns us in James 3: 1-8 (KJV), *"My brethren, be not many masters, knowing that we shall receive the greater condemnation. For in many things we offend all. If any man offend not in word, the same is a perfect man, and able also to bridle the whole body. Behold, we put bits in the horses mouths, that they may obey us; and we turn about their whole body. Behold also the ships, which though they be so great, and are driven of fierce winds, yet are they turned about with a very small helm, whithersoever the governor listeth. Even so the tongue is a little member, and boasteth great things. Behold how great a matter a little fire kindleth! And the tongue is a fire, a world of iniquity: so is the tongue among our members, that it defileth the whole body, and setteth on fire the course of nature;*

and it is set on fire of hell. For every kind of beasts, and of birds, and of serpents, and of things in the sea, is tamed, and hath been tamed of mankind: But the tongue can no man tame; it is an unruly evil, full of deadly poison."

As Christians we have a responsibility to listen for the voice of the Lord and wait for his instructions opposed to taking matters into our own hands. If we are obedient to the command of the Lord and learn how to deny ourselves in order to allow the Holy Spirit to increase and manifest itself within us, the title will quickly transform from "Lord, I'll take it from here," into "Lord, Strong Deliverer, Be Thou Still my Strength and Shield."

From the center and from Left to right in the rear: Kelvin D. Bodley, Laura Velez and Harland Bradley complete documentation to file lawsuit against county for racial discrimination and retaliation

Chapter Ten

How To Prepare For A Legal Battle While On Your Job

I have learned through my personal trials and tribulations that experience is the best teacher. Often I have observed co-workers closing their eyes and ignoring the injustice of racism and retaliation within the workplace? As, I pose this question, you must first open your eyes and conduct a self examination and count the times you heard of an incident or witnessed a co-workers civil rights being violated by management or other co-workers and you quietly turned around and walked the other way.

In many instances, we have adopted the world's theory of saving ourselves regardless of what happens around us. People have used this argument that you can't help anyone until you first help yourself. Consequently, this theory makes good sense if you ignore all Biblical principals of putting it all in God's hands and realize that promotion doesn't come from the east or the west, but from the Lord who made heaven and earth. In other words, we are our brother's keeper.

Although I never met those countless activists who marched during the struggle, went to prison, made tremendous sacrifices and died for freedom and equal opportunity, those who were Christians understood the importance of faith and relied on God's promise regardless of the consequences.

Unfortunately, many of today's modern Christians must experience a crisis before they truly become awakened to their circumstances and realize, if they choose to hide beneath their desk and close their eyes, eventually they too will encounter trouble on their job.

Many of us have witnessed and experienced racism or other forms of discrimination on the job; we often find more reasons to either ignore the problem because our fear of retaliation or we simply pray the Lord will deliver us from evil with another job or better yet, a winning lottery ticket.

The question we must ask ourselves, what happens when you experience trouble on the job? The voice of the Lord said after you've done all you can do, stand? Before we can address this question, let me give you a pop quiz to determine if you should consider early retirement, increase your dosage of morphine, see a psychiatrist or prepare for a legal battle while on your job.

1. What is your skill level as it relates to computer technology and work experience?
2　What are your educational credentials? Do you have any certifications, and special licenses?
3. Has your annual performance evaluation been bad, mediocre, or good?
4. Has your supervisor ever issued any disciplinary or corrective action against you regardless if the allegations were substantiated?
5. How good is your grammar and do you have problems composing a memorandum?
6. Do you have affidavits or documentation of any correspondence that supports your allegations?
7. Do you prepare weekly summary reports to your supervisor or prepare summaries of your meetings to the attendees for record purposes?

8. Do you prepare minutes of your discussions with co-workers or business associates?
9. Do you know what's in your personnel file?
10. How would your case make a difference for others in the workplace should you prevail in your lawsuit?

The ten questions referenced in the quiz are a small snap shot of what is essential for you to prepare for battle within the workplace. It's important never to let a situation dictate your response. For instance, most of us have witnessed co-workers angry about how unjustly they were treated in the workplace. They reacted by demonstrating their frustration through their emotional verbal rhetoric. Consequently, management quickly responded by issuing disciplinary action with the intent of setting an example for all to see.

A hostile working environment can be everyone's worse nightmare. Unfortunately, many employees underestimate the options available to management in an effort to eliminate their job and justify it through the camouflage of a legitimate business decision. As a result, many people try to battle this pattern of injustice by channeling their emotions and compassionate opinions believing the truth will ultimately surface; however, truth must be birthed with the burden of proof which comes from factual documentation.

Furthermore, before preparing for a legal battle on the job, don't forget to review these five critical points:

1. Familiarize yourself with the personnel policy manual to determine what your rights are as an employee.
2. It's imperative to assess your environment and rank how you compare to your co-workers as it relates to experience, educational credentials, job classification and salary.

3. Develop a chronology of events reaffirming your allegations and establishing a timeline.
4. Documentation, documentation, documentation always validates facts and supersedes opinion regardless of your compassion.
5. Friends might have good intentions, but it is rare they will put their livelihood on the line to validate your allegations.

The Apostle Paul wrote in the book of Ephesians 6:10-19, (KJV), *Finally, my brethren, be strong in the Lord, and in the power of his might. Put on the whole Armour of God that ye may be able to stand against the wiles of the devil. For we wrestle not against flesh and blood, but against principalities, against powers, against the rulers of the darkness of this world, against spiritual wickedness in high places. Wherefore take unto you the whole Armor of God that ye may be able to withstand in the evil day, and having done all, to stand. Stand therefore, having your loins girt about with truth, and having on the breastplate of righteousness; And your feet shod with the preparation of the gospel of peace; Above all, taking the shield of faith, wherewith ye shall be able to quench all the fiery darts of the wicked. And take the helmet of salvation, and the sword of the Spirit, which is the word of God: Praying always with all prayer and supplication in the Spirit, and watching thereunto with all perseverance and supplication for all saints; And for me, that utterance may be given unto me, that I may open my mouth boldly, to make known the mystery of the gospel, For which I am an ambassador in bonds: that therein I may speak boldly, as I ought to speak.*

Chapter Eleven

How Does One Determine If Their Legal Council Is Friend Or Foe?

—∽∽—

We are in a society where people find themselves seeking legal counsel for various reasons. There are numerous cases where attorneys have demonstrated their commitment and dedication towards serving as a legal agent on behalf of their client; however, there are other instances where some attorneys either utilize their knowledge of the law to take advantage of their client and the judicial system or fail to have the adequate knowledge and time necessary to properly defend their client. Unfortunately, many people take for granted the attorney they select or appointed by the courts to represent them will conduct themselves in an ethical manner required by the law.

Jesus demonstrated in Matthew 27: 17-19, (KJV), although Pontius Pilate was responsible for administering justice and upholding the Roman law, which said an innocent man should not be put to death, Pontius Pilate was more concerned about political expediency and what the crowd would think of him if he ignored their wishes to crucify an innocent man opposed to upholding the Roman law.

Many of us can't imagine what it would be like if we were forced to defend ourselves on our job. In many instances, people get frustrated when the system fails to protect their civil rights and they look for ways to escape by finding new employment opportunities; unfortunately, the problem perpetuates and eventually swallows up more defenseless victims. On the other hand, a small minority actually exercises their legal rights by filing a lawsuit against the establishment; however, when that major decision is made to pursue legal action and hire an attorney, countless people instantly activate the auto pilot switch and rely solely on the attorney's guidance without verifying the facts or other legal options. As a result, the client find themselves going on an expensive journey based solely on the word of their legal counsel without validating the facts by conducting additional research.

Some attorneys will inform you at the beginning of the case that there are no guarantees the outcome will be in your favor regardless of the facts. It's important to remember in a court of law a lot of variables are contributing factors towards the outcome of the case. For instance, if a client has filed a Civil Rights lawsuit in the area of racial discrimination and retaliation, the Judge assigned to the case could have a history of ruling against civil rights cases. As a result, the client could easily find themselves with a Summary Judgment ruling against their complaint regardless of the facts and are left in a position to pay additional money and file an appeal in hopes of having the initial ruling overturned by a higher court. It's important to note that in the appeals process; only 13% of the cases are actually overturned by a higher court.

There are situations on the job that many of us have encountered showing evidence and patterns of discrimination. Although we finally make the difficult decision to exercise our civil rights by pursuing legal action against the employer, we sometimes fail to conduct a thorough search towards selecting a qualified attorney to represent our best legal interest.

Before a client can began to examine the necessary criteria to determine if their attorney is a friend or foe, they must first establish a foundation and assess the qualifications of the attorney that best meets their needs. The following ten steps will help you identify a qualified attorney to represent your case:

1. Contact the Bar Association and request the names of attorneys that are licensed in Civil Rights and/or Employment Discrimination
2. Research the Internet for law firms and request the names and resumes of attorneys in the field of interest.
3. Inquire from friends or associates that have knowledge of reputable attorneys.
4. Prioritize the list of candidates and contact them to determine if they own or work for a small or large law firm.
5. Find out the number of support staff available for research and if the law firm provides copies of all correspondence to the client.
6. Request information regarding the track record of similar cases handled by the legal candidate and evaluates the number of wins verses losses.
7. Determine the fee schedule and if the attorney will take your case on contingency.
8. Discuss the projected timetable regarding this case and request an explanation of what to expect as an employee once you file the lawsuit.
9. Find out what type of documentation the attorney will require to affirm your lawsuit.
10. Ask the attorney to provide an assessment of your case and to determine the probability of winning summary judgment.

Once you identify an attorney, the most significant assessment for the client to make is determining if your attorney is a friend or foe? The worst feeling a client can have after filing a lawsuit against their employer, they have spent most of their time and hard earned or borrowed money arguing with the attorney in an attempt to affirm their case. Although the attorney is required to focus on the aspects of the law and how the facts of the case relate to the law, the attorney should also spend as much energy trying to understand the facts of the case through the eyes of the client.

Many people don't realize attorneys often have numerous clients they represent regardless of the size of the law firm. As a result, clients don't always receive the quality time necessary to properly prepare for the case.

For instance, when you begin to count the number of clients, trial briefs, discovery, notice of filing, depositions, counseling sessions, and legal documents that must be filed to adhere to the court schedule, it doesn't leave a lot of quality time to shoot the breeze with your attorney. Most importantly, if you are not organized and fails to demonstrate knowledge regarding your legal rights, they can help contribute towards their attorney failing to adequately represent you.

In order to avoid the pitfall of your attorney becoming a foe, you have a responsibility to hold them accountable to meet the following criteria:

1. Make sure your attorney educates you about the facts of the case and how the law applies.
2. Have your attorney provide a thorough counseling session on how workplaces conduct once you file the lawsuit.
3. Be sure your attorney shows you the entire process as it relates to requirements by the attorney and the court in order to win summary judgment.

4. Make sure your attorney listens and values your opinion.
5. Make sure your attorney permits you to review all legal documents prior to filing them with the court and that they are filed in a timely manner to meet the required court deadlines.
6. Always discuss the proper conduct on how to handle yourself when preparing for depositions.
7. Have your attorney review the financial liability and alert you of the financial risk that could occur in the event you lose the case.
8. Ask your attorney for a reasonable pay schedule to avoid inflated legal bills.
9. Have your attorney review the significance of a settlement in the event opposing counsel wants to reach an agreement during mediation.
10. Make sure your attorney provides extensive research to find case law that supports your argument in preparation for trial.

In the event your attorney appears to have "foe" like symptoms and is too busy or insensitive towards you, it is best to take immediate action and terminate the attorney and search for new legal counsel. As a client, never permit the attorney to hold you hostage or surrender your integrity because the attorney failed to represent you properly. On the other hand, a good attorney will inspire confidence in their client by demonstrating knowledge of the law, as well as illustrate compassion and conviction towards seeking justice on behalf of their client.

Finally, as you have become more knowledgeable of your case and understand the risks that are involved, make sure you don't underestimate the importance of having family support. Your family will be the lifeline towards determining how long you can endure this arduous battle against a system that has unlimited financial resources. Regardless of the facts, you can be put in unbearable circumstances by the system in hopes of forcing the clients to resign or conduct themselves in an unprofessional manner, which could lead to termination.

King Solomon wrote in the book of Proverbs 2:6-11, (KJV), *For the Lord gives wisdom; from His mouth come knowledge and understanding; He stores up sound wisdom for the upright; He is a shield to those who walk uprightly; He guards the paths of justice, and preserves the way of His saints. Then you will understand righteousness and justice, Equity and every good path. When wisdom enters your heart and knowledge is pleasant to your soul; Discretion will preserve you; Understanding will keep you.*

Kelvin D. Bodley slips into deep meditation as he reached his breaking point during his long arduous battle of discrimination against the county

Chapter Twelve

BREAKING----------POINT

So they sat down with him upon the ground seven days and seven nights and none spake a word unto him: for they saw his grief was very great. After this opened Job his mouth, and cursed his day. And Job spake, and said, Let the day perish wherein I was born, and the night in which it was said, there is a man child conceived. **Job 2: 13; 3:1-3 (KJV)**

The Lord was merely exercising his bragging rights on his servant Job when he granted Satan permission to test Job by removing His hedge of protection. During Job's journey of long suffering, Satan attacked his character, destroyed his property, killed his children and caused painful boils from the sole of his feet to the crown of his head with the intention of consuming Job for good measure. Job had clearly experienced countless calamities with his personal bout with Satan. He appeared to have finally reached his breaking point when he cursed the very day he was born. Nevertheless, Job sinned not, nor did he charge God foolishly or curse God as a result of his painful tribulations.

Most of us could probably never imagine enduring a fraction of Job's journey through the valley of shadow of death. If we were to be honest with ourselves, we would probably ask the Lord to remain humble and stop bragging to Satan about our character in hopes of avoiding such an encounter. However, if an examination was conducted on our character and integrity in the workplace, Satan would be running to the Lord exercising his bragging rights about the disharmony many of us have displayed amongst one another as Christians.

When was the last time you had a moment to reflect on your most recent encounter in your place of employment that made you so angry that you shared the passion and thoughts of Job, and cursed the day you were born? I often reflect on my personal experiences as an African-American male in a world where many have refused to accept me as an equal regardless of my educational credentials and contributions as a professional within the workplace. Consequently, the struggles of racial discrimination and retaliation that many of us face in the workplace appear to be a natural part of our journey as professionals regardless of our credentials.

There were countless times when I became dishearten with the system that was determined to alienate me and demonstrate it with noticeable patterns of racial discrimination and retaliation demonstrated by management and fellow co-workers. However, the greatest frustration resulted from dealing with my own fellow brothers and sisters in Christ who chose to murmur amongst themselves opposed to working together and allowing our lights to shine before man so they can see our good works. My brothers and sisters in Christ could have given God the glory had they simply prayed for courage and direction to address the wanton patterns of discrimination. Instead of serving as a beacon of hope and reaching out with words of encouragement and comfort, they soon became silent and immediately distanced themselves from me to avoid any association as though I had been diagnosed with leprosy. It was apparent the invisible walls of silence sent a message that was loud and clear for everyone to stay away from me if they valued their professional careers.

I better understood the impact of my Job-like experience when I realized that despite having a Bachelor of Science degree in Business Management, a Masters degree in the field of Public Administration and over twenty years of experience in my profession and operated the number one customer service center within my division; nevertheless, I was still not considered an equal among my white colleagues. The non African-American supervisors in my division were not required to meet the minimum qualifications for their positions. In fact, not one of those non-African American supervisors possessed a college degree since the inception of the Code Enforcement Division; nevertheless, I was the lowest paid supervisor within the division.

Before I could wake up from this terrible nightmare, there came another messenger unto me, reminding me when I filed a complaint with the county's Office of Professional Standards in an effort to investigate my allegations of racial discrimination and retaliation. The Office of Professional Standards only interviewed two out of eight of my witnesses and dismissed the complaint for lack of evidence; where as, when a white co-worker conspired with management and filed a complaint against me for creating a hostile work environment, the Office of Professional Standards interviewed 13 witnesses in regards to the case. Fortunately, the allegations were later proven to be unsubstantiated since I was able to provide documentation to prove the co-worker was deceptive and permitted herself to be used as a pawn in a system that was determine to destroy my character by building a case against me.

Before I could convince my colleagues that I was not obsessed with my concerns, there came another messenger unto me, reminding me how I tried to point out in a report that an Office of Professional Standards white investigator conspired with the white manager of the Code Enforcement Division by altering a July 2, 2003 Sworn Statement to assure a favorable outcome regarding the investigation. The Sworn Statement confirmed although the interview was conducted on July 2, 2003, the manager and the investigator were discussing events that occurred on July 11, 2003. Evidence clearly proved unless they were prophets and able to see into the future, they fabricated the facts of the case in an effort to destroy the professional careers of myself and anyone else that supported the allegations of racial discrimination and retaliation against the county.

Once the evidence was brought to the attention of the legal council representing the county, they offered to pay a settlement in the amount of $10,000 which I quickly rejected. Nevertheless, despite a wanton pattern of corruption that occurred between the manager and the investigator, no disciplinary action ever occurred and they both continue to interview and investigate claims of employees seeking justice within an organization that protects it self through fraudulent behavior and overt tactics.

While I was reflecting on the injustices that have all but consumed me with consternation and frustration, it appeared as though I had slipped into a deep state of unconsciousness and there came a messenger unto me, reminding me how I and the other African American supervisor in the division had been excluded from participating in supervisory meetings with management for over a year and a half; however, the white Manager met with the non African-American supervisors on a regular basis.

Before I could even begin to grasp my thoughts surrounding this "Black-Out," there came another messenger unto me, reminding me of the evidence confirmed during my deposition when the African American Director made the recommendation to the County Administration for me to be considered for the Assistant Manager position in the

Code Enforcement Division. The County Administrator was determined not to permit that to happen under any circumstances. As a result, despite the Assistant Manager position being budgeted since the inception of the Code Enforcement Division and employed two previous whites as Assistant Managers prior to my consideration, the County Administration Office ultimately made the decision not to advertise the Assistant Manager position, which has been vacant to date since March of 2002.

Most importantly, to assure the deceptive practices continued and that I would never be afforded that opportunity to further my professional career, the county permitted the manager in the Code Enforcement Division to recently advertise a Chief Inspector position to replace the vacant Assistant Manager position. Consequently, the Chief Inspector would assume all of the duties outlined in the original Assistant Manager Job description and afford the Chief Inspector the authority to serve as Manager in his absence as outlined in the February 5, 2006 job posting. Ironically, the African American Director argued during my deposition that the Chief Inspector position never existed; however, we later proved the African American Director lied when we produced evidence of a Code Enforcement budget outlining the new duties of the Chief Inspector position; thus, confirming the county was determined to eliminate any possibility that I would become the first African American Assistant Manager for the Code Enforcement Division.

Before I could scream towards the heavens above regarding the gross injustice, there came another messenger unto me, reminding me that although I had submitted various complaints to management and administrators regarding the reckless behavior of exclusion and discrimination towards my staff, no investigations or corrective action ever were initiated by the County Administration or lower level management.

Before I realized the full impact of how many employees were afraid to speak out against the problems that were ramped within County Government, there came another messenger unto me, reminding me how evidence confirmed a white supervisor for the Code Enforcement Division falsified his educational credentials on his employment application. Although the employee indicated that he possessed an Associates degree and a Bachelors of Arts degree in the field of criminal justice, evidence confirmed he never received a certificate of diplomacy from an accredited university. Nevertheless, the County Administration and upper management within the Code Enforcement Division ignored the allegations and permitted the supervisor to remain in his current status to date. Where as, an employment background check revealed an African American who was hired as a Code Enforcement Officer falsified his employment credentials during the application process. However, once the fraudulent activity was discovered by the white manager, the African American was terminated immediately.

Before I reached my breaking point, there came another messenger unto me, reminding me as a result of my complaints, the Code Enforcement Division was conveniently restructured and the section that I supervised was eliminated as a result of automation and new technology. Even though my section was referenced as a model by the County to emulate for providing quality customer service, the staff that supported my allegations of racial discrimination was transferred to the Call Center to answer telephones, and I was transferred to another division with no supervisory status or upper mobility. On the other hand, two of the remaining staff that did not support my allegations was permitted to remain within the Code Enforcement Division under another supervisor. More over, the Code Enforcement Division had immediately reassigned our "obsolete" duties under the supervision of a white supervisor who currently performs the same "obsolete" functions to the Board of County Commissioners, Chairman and County Administration office today.

Therefore, my dear brother and sister in Christ stay encouraged and understand the problem that often occurs in situations of discrimination when the system perpetuates fear into employees, particularly when there is an abuse of power. Many people will settle for a career of lateral mobility and job security oppose to accepting the consequences as a result of challenging a corrupt political system of Government. As you may be aware, management swiftly harasses most employees who dare to display courage against an unjust system and their character is ultimately assassinated. Sooner or later, the employee's name is slandered throughout the system as though it were a public lynching. As a result, the employee is quickly labeled angry, too emotional or a troublemaker through methods of collusion by the system and eventually the employee is forced to be transferred to a less desirable employment assignment, resign, or eventually terminated. Nevertheless, God promised never to leave us or forsake us regardless of the circumstances.

After experiencing tremendous sorrow and regretting the day that I was born, the Lord reminded me what Paul said in II Corinthians 12: 10 (KJV), *"Therefore, I take pleasure in infirmities, in reproaches, in necessities, in persecutions, in distresses for Christ's sake: for when I am weak, then am I strong."* As a result, I made the commitment to put my entire trust in the Lord despite the circumstances. I realized the Lord was affording me the opportunity to make a spiritual break through beyond my breaking point in order to walk through this unknown journey of hatred by faith and not by sight.

Kelvin D. Bodley refused to surrender to the retaliation tactics by the county and was determined to rely on the principles of Christ regardless of the professional and legal consequences that awaited him

Chapter Thirteen

No Man Can Hinder Me

Strengthen you the weak hands, and confirm the feeble knees. Say to them that are of a fearful heart, Be strong, fear not: behold your God will come with vengeance, even God with a recompense; He will come and save you. Then the eyes of the blind shall be opened, and the ears of the deaf shall be unstopped. And a highway shall be there, and a way, and it shall be called the way of holiness; the unclean shall not pass over it; but it shall be for those: the wayfaring men, though fools, shall not err therein. Isaiah 35: 3-5,8, (KJV)

I was inspired to write these words of encouragement after reading the book entitled "No Man Can Hinder Me" by the author, Ms. Velma Maia Thomas who eloquently retraced our ancestor's journey from slavery to emancipation through songs. The songs provided strength for slaves to trust in the Lord and carry on despite unbearable circumstances they endured as they struggled and died for their freedom. After staggering through my personal journey of modern day slavery as a government employee, I painfully recognized that racial discrimination was very much alive and merely masqueraded with the sheet of haughtiness and cowardice.

Although there were countless nights when I felt as though I cried my last tears due to the frustration of working within an entangled bureaucratic and supercilious system of duplicity; I was determined to hold onto God's unchanging hand to lead me through one of the most difficult encounters within my short existence upon this earth. I cannot begin to describe how my personal life was ripped into shreds before my very eyes; my character was dismantled with constant scrutiny from colleagues, associates and upper level management labeling me as obsessed, bitter and reckless without regards for others.

As a result, there were innumerable occasions when I began to question myself and ponder whether the struggle for justice was merely an illusion or a horrible exercise in futility. I glaringly recall the excruciating process of being diagnosed like a laboratory animal in a science class by the opposing legal counsel during my June 11, 2003 deposition. This grueling procedure was designed to break my spirit by wearing me down both mentally and physically through attrition in an effort to generate inconsistent statements for the purpose of dismantling my credibility.

However, the Lord reaffirmed His presence with me at the seventh hour when the court reporter burst out with a loud shout that she couldn't take the process any further and wanted to know how much longer the deposition would continue. As a result, in an effort to calm the court reporter's shattered nerves, the opposing legal counsel reluctantly responded to her by saying, a half hour;

The deposition continued for another two hours. Nevertheless, the Lord had renewed my strength by revealing to me that the end of this arduous process was near.

Even though the deposition lasted for almost ten hours and appeared to slowly drag into eternity; The Lord clearly embraced me with the declaration of truth as He brought to my remembrance the words that Moses prayed as a man of

God: *He that dwells in the secret place of the Most High shall abide under the shadow of the Almighty. I will say of the Lord, He is my refuge and my fortress: my God; in Him will I trust. Surely He shall deliver you from the snare of the fowler, and from the noisome pestilence. He shall cover you with His feathers, and under His wings shall you trust: His truth shall be your shield and buckler.* Psalm 91:1-4 (KJV)

Unfortunately, many of my proud colleagues failed to understand why I sounded the trumpet of racial discrimination and jeopardized my professional career. Consequently, they appeared to be more concerned that my actions and allegations of discrimination could possibly hinder their lateral mobility as a result of challenging the stalwart powers within county government. More over, many of my colleagues refused to comprehend that my conviction was based on spiritual fortitude and the value to stand for what was right in the eyes of God opposed towards the fear losing my job. Nevertheless, it was imperative that I relied on my faith and trust in the Lord to guide my foot steps and to lead me through the dark and lonely valley of employment discrimination.

Many of my proud colleagues failed to understand why I sounded the trumpet of racial discrimination when I filed a complaint against the Honorable Judge G. Kendall Sharp regarding the integrity of the order rendered in my case. At the time of my deposition, Orange County's legal council arrogantly bragged during their opening statements about having the Honorable G. Kendall Sharp serve as the presiding Judge in this case as a result of his reputation for ruling against civil rights cases. In addition, the Mediator and my legal council both confirmed the reputation established by Honorable Judge G. Kendall Sharp. Further more, I spoke to several attorneys who indicated that civil rights cases ruled on by Judge Sharp often are dismissed in summary judgment despite the facts in the case.

Many of my proud colleagues failed to understand why I sounded the trumpet of racial discrimination when a letter of determination was issued from the Equal Employment Opportunity Commission for employment discrimination, retaliation and constructive discharge for two of my staff. Evidence confirmed both staff members were retaliated against by management for serving as a witness on my behalf for filing a lawsuit against county government. As a result, county government would deny any hint of guilt towards the cruel charges, but offered a financial settlement agreement per person to withdraw their claim and to sign a statement agreeing to no longer work for county government.

Consequently, after experiencing three exhausting years of retaliation and to avoid any further emotional strain on their family and professional careers, both staff members accepted the financial settlements in an effort to begin the lengthy journey of re-assembling their shattered lives.

Many of my proud colleagues failed to understand why I sounded the trumpet of racial discrimination when county government ignored my documented evidence of record and attempted to silence me by imposing their legal fees in the amount of $227,000. Their goal was to conduct a personal lynching and display me as an example for others to witness this costly battle against injustice. Although I seriously considered filing bankruptcy to avoid them collecting one red cent, I maintained my sanity and spiritual compass and made a business decision. I reluctantly agreed to pay $25,000.00 to avoid the entire legal liability. Despite the fact that I incurred personal legal expenses that exceeded $75,000.00, I firmly believe the Lord ordered my steps to stand against the wiles of the devil.

Many of my proud colleagues failed to understand why I sounded the trumpet of racial discrimination and retaliation in my pursuit for equality, fairness and justice under a system of government that is over seen by leadership which demonstrates questionable ethics and integrity through their actions. For example, the Orlando Sentinel reported an article, Sunday, March 19, 2006, written by David Damron and Roger Roy as Sentinel staff writers entitled, "Crotty partner got county OK." In my estimation, the article simply confirmed what I personally experienced and demonstrated how easy it is to watch evidence evaporate before your very eyes or ears as in this case, when the article reported that "The reasons for reversal on a strip mall are unclear, staff won't talk and meeting tapes are blank."

The article stated, "At a time when he was in a lucrative land partnership with Orange County Mayor Rich Crotty, a prominent developer got the go-ahead from the county staff to build a controversial shopping center that the staff had earlier opposed. The county staff's approval of the shopping center proposed by developer Daryl Carter in west Orange County in 2003 came as Carter and Crotty were in the midst of South Florida land deal in which Crotty made $112,000 – and which is now being investigated by a special prosecutor. The go-ahead for the shopping center after Carter purchased the site was a reversal of the staff's earlier statements that the project departed from the county's development rules, the Orlando Sentinel has found."

In my opinion, this article appeared to shine a huge spot light in the corners of darkness and unravel allegations of back room deals that have gone on for centuries. The article went on to say, "And tape recordings of one key county staff meeting at which Carter's shopping-center development was discussed, obtained by the Sentinel through the state's public-records laws, are blank. County officials said such technical failures were not unusual with the equipment it had at the time. Despite such gaps in the record of how the county handled Carter's development, the available public records underscore the potential for the appearance of conflicts of interest in the mayor's yearlong private partnership with a prominent developer."

Even though my supporters and I were ostracized by the entire management group in county government, I felt compelled to sound the trumpet for justice and fairness within a conservative court system in hopes of putting an end to the unfair and detrimental practices permitted by county government. After experiencing an internal assassination on my character and professional career, my personal life will forever be altered and scarred with the deep lacerations of racial discrimination and retaliation. Nevertheless, I am reminded of the Psalm of David, when he said, *Fret not yourself because of evil doers, neither be you envious against the workers of iniquity. For they shall soon be cut down like grass, and wither as the green herb. Trust in the Lord, and do good; so shall you dwell in the land, and verily you shall be fed. Delight yourself also in the Lord; and He shall give you the desires of your heart. Commit your way to the Lord; trust also in Him; and He shall bring it to pass. And He shall bring forth your righteousness as the light, and your judgment as the noonday. Rest in the Lord, and wait patiently for him: fret not yourself because of him who prospers in his way, because of the man who brings wicked devices to pass. Cease from anger, and forsake wrath: fret not yourself in any wise to do evil. For evildoers shall be cut off: but those that wait upon the lord, they shall inherit the earth.* Psalm 37: 1-9 (KJV)

Chapter Fourteen

Hello Lord, "Are You Still There?"

"*Why standest thou afar off, O Lord? Why hidest thou thyself in times of trouble? The wicked in his place doth persecute the poor: let them be taken in the devices that they have imagined. For the wicked boasteth of his heart's desire, and blesseth the covetous, whom the Lord abhorreth. The wicked, through the pride of his countenance, will not seek after God: God is not in all his thoughts. His ways are always grievous; thy judgments are far above out of his sight: as for all his enemies, he puffeth at them. He hath said in his heart, I shall not be moved: for I shall never be in adversity. His mouth is full of cursing and deceit and fraud: under his tongue is mischief and vanity. He sitteth in the lurking places of the villages: in the secret places doth he murder the innocent: his eyes are privily set against the poor. He lieth in wait secretly as a lion in his den: he lieth in wait to catch the poor: he doth catch him into his net. He croucheth, and humbleth himself, that the poor may fall by his strong ones. He hath said in his heart, God hath forgotten: he hideth his face; he will never see it. Arise, O Lord: O God, lift up thine hand: forget not the humble.*"(Psalm 10: 1-12 KJV)

The Boiling Pot of Injustice

David asked the question, why do the wicked appear to succeed? Although David felt as though the Lord was far away, he never stopped praying or came to the conclusion that the Lord did not care for him or his circumstances. David simply wanted the Lord to hurry to his aid. It is a natural response, when we are in trouble, to tell the Lord about our trials and seek immediate relief from our situation immediately. When was the last time you attempted to hide in an effort to escape from the trials and tribulations that knocked on your door? Have you ever experienced crying out to the Lord seeking an answer and all you received in response was total silence?

There were countless times, I wondered if the Lord had merely forgotten that he had left me in the hands of my enemy just a little bit longer than he intended? As a result, I began to doubt myself and started to question my faith and wondered if the Lord was simply teaching me a lesson? I remember, all of those times I cut vacation bible school and ventured to the game room; maybe the Lord was still mad at me for keeping some of the money my parents had given me for church and I used it to buy a hoagie sandwich with hot peppers? Maybe the Lord wasn't pleased with me for taking the church flowers donated by various auxiliaries from the altar and giving them to my girlfriend's parents after church? Whatever the case, I began to reflect on all the trouble that I have caused and pleaded to the Lord for his bountiful mercy and grace.

As I continued to conduct a self-examination of myself, I started slipping into a pattern of uncertainty, which forced me to reflect back on my personal experience with employment discrimination as an African American supervisor. I started to convince myself that I had enough courage to question the Lord, so I began to get a running start and shouted at the top of my lungs, "Hello Lord, are you still there?" Even though I understood when the Apostle Paul wrote, *Romans 5: 1-5,*

(KJV), "Therefore being justified by faith, we have peace with God through our Lord Jesus Christ: By whom also we have access by faith into this grace wherein we stand, and rejoice in hope of the glory of God. And not only so, but we glory in tribulations also: knowing that tribulation worketh patience; And patience, experience; and experience hope: And hope maketh not ashamed; because the love of God is shed abroad in our hearts by the Holy Ghost which is given unto us."

Nevertheless, it was difficult rejoicing in the midst of racial discrimination within an organized establishment that policed itself and demonstrated a consistent pattern of promoting only one African American at a time in the upper county administrative level of management. "Hello Lord, are you still there?"

It was difficult rejoicing after sending supportive documentation validating reckless patterns of discrimination to the Board of County Commissioners and the upper county administrative level of management, only for them to ignore my track record of professionalism and refuse to conduct an independent investigation; thus, closing their eyes towards the constant patterns of retaliation and discriminatory practices rendered by management. "Hello Lord, are you still there?"

It was difficult rejoicing after providing facts and documentation to legal counsel, then going almost ten hours in my deposition, and spending my life savings and incurring enormous legal expenditures in pursuit of justice within a corrupt system of government only to be accused of being an angry black man with a senseless point to prove. "Hello Lord, are you still there?"

It was difficult rejoicing when my marriage experienced the deep lacerations of frustration and fear as a result of my decision to stand against spiritual wickedness in high places by pursuing a lawsuit against county government for racial discrimination and retaliation. As a result, the shattered fragments of discrimination ultimately overwhelm us and fostered a painful atmosphere of separatism and resentment for threatening our home and creating financial instability. "Hello Lord, are you still there?"

It was difficult rejoicing after complaining to some of the African American politicians, local grass roots organizations, and African American news media regarding our concerns; yet, no one appeared to understand the urgency that plagued many of their brothers and sisters in Christ pleading for an investigation in an effort to expose the gratuitous pattern of hatred and discrimination.

Where do you go when everyone appears to be in hiding to avoid the political consequences should they address the issues of injustice? Most employees are a payroll check away from disaster should they face such an unbearable endeavor of challenging an established system that abuses tax payers dollars to suppress the truth. I've witnessed African American employees paralyzed against an organization that focuses on discrediting individuals that appear to have valid claims of discrimination. Unfortunately, depending on where you live in the region can make the difference between organizations standing up and fighting against the injustices that plague minorities or merely remaining silent and permitting the cancer of destruction to perpetuate and ultimately suppress a people.

Regrettably, some of the African American churches and local grass roots organizations have been toothless and pose absolutely no threat towards holding a corrupt organization accountable for their illicit actions. As a result, the established organization often uses the employee as an example and performs a modern day lynching to alert everyone else of the consequences should they venture off the plantation.

Therefore, it is my appeal to reach out to the African American churches across the land and request assistance for those employees in your congregation that need help while experiencing discrimination within the workplace.

Many of the African American churches have their own legal counsel (attorney, judges, etc) worshipping at their churches that could provide direction and support to the least of God's children. Spiritual and legal counsel could be instrumental towards educating their brothers and sisters in Christ regarding employment discrimination and retaliation while standing on the word of God.

Finally, the church can also serve as a liaison on behalf of the employee and address the critical issues that often are ignored by an established organization due to the failure of facing a possible consequence from the spiritual community should they not comply. The Apostle Paul wrote: Ephesians 6: 10-12 (KJV), *"Finally, my brethren, be strong in the Lord, and in the power of his might. Put on the armor of God that ye may be able to stand against the wiles of the devil. For we wrestle not against flesh and blood, but against principalities, against powers, against rulers of the darkness of this world, against spiritual wickedness in high places."*

Kelvin D. Bodley understood the importance
relying on his faith and trust in God while he held onto
the promises of Christ regardless of the high ways
of despair that he endured through the painful
discrimination journey.

Chapter Fifteen

Shout WITH A Victory

The Psalm writer wrote in Psalm 98:1-9; (KJV), *O sing unto the Lord a new song; for he hath done marvelous things: His right hand, and His holy arm, has gotten Him the victory. The Lord hath made known his salvation: His righteousness has He openly showed in the sight of the heathen. He has remembered His mercy and His truth toward the house of Israel: all the ends of the earth have seen the salvation of our God. Make a joyful noise unto the Lord, all the earth: make a loud noise, and rejoice, and sing praise. Sing unto the Lord with the harp; with the harp, and the voice of a psalm. With trumpets and sound of cornet make a joyful noise before the Lord, the King. Let the sea roar, and the fullness thereof; the world, and they that dwell therein. Let the floods clap their hands: let the hills be joyful together before the Lord; for He comes to judge the earth: with righteousness shall he judge the world, and the people with equity.*

Regardless of the trials and tribulations that await those of us who choose to stand against discrimination and injustice within the workplace, the Lord will grant the ultimate victory to them that have suffered afflictions for His name sake. Therefore, despite the worldly gains of discrimination, **"Shout with a Victory"** and begin singing a song of praise while relying on the promises of Christ. There were many days and sleepless nights when my spirit was consumed with heartache during my walk through the valley of the shadow of employment discrimination; nevertheless, I forced myself to scrape the depths of my soul in hopes of finding any residue of a song that would comfort and reinvigorate my battered spirit.

I came to the realization that no matter how desperately I tried to reassemble the fragmented pieces of my broken character that was kicked around by the harden boots of hatred and arrogance; I had all but given up any hope of ever receiving any resolve or assistance from anyone regarding this senseless voyage of racial discrimination and retaliation. After realizing that I could not take another step and needed Jesus to carry me, I recall falling to my knees one late midnight hour and reciting the song written by Judson W. Van De Venter and Winfield S. Weeden, entitled, "I Surrender All." *All to Jesus I surrender, All to HIM I freely give, I will ever love and trust Him, In His presence daily live; All to Jesus I surrender, Humbly at His feet I bow; worldly pleasures all forsaken, take me, Jesus, take me know; All to Jesus I surrender, Make me, Savior, wholly Thine, Let me feel the Holy Spirit Truly know that Thou art mine; All to Jesus I surrender, Lord, I give myself to Thee, Fill me with thy love and power, let thy blessings fall on me; I surrender all, I surrender all, I surrender all, all to Thee, my blessed Savior, I surrender all.*

Even though I came to grips with toiling through the anguish of this horrific journey, it wasn't until I witnessed many of my colleagues and friends evaporate into thin air right before my very eyes that I was awakened to the harsh realities of fear. As a result, doubt quickly began to penetrate the open wounds resulting from my decision to stand on the principles of Christ against an arrogant system of absolute power. There was no mistake that all eyes were watching my every step as I move throughout the Administration building to carry out my daily duties. I felt as though a bounty was placed on my head and it was merely a matter of time before the retaliatory tactics of exclusion and harassment would overwhelm me and the few staff and fellow co-workers that had the courage to stand along my side.

Nevertheless, I truly thank God for the prayers and words of encouragement from my family, and dearest friends during one of the most difficult experiences of my life. Despite feeling abandoned by an unjust system, my parents often reminded me of the importance of prayer and to always rely on the promises of Christ regardless of the consequences. As a child, my parents took the time to teach me the importance of kneeling and communing with our Father in heaven and telling Him all about our troubles, because they understood that He is a burden bearer and a bridge over troubled water. My parents took the time to teach me about the importance of having faith, because He is Jehovah-Jireh, my provider; Jehovah Nissi, my battle fighter; Jehovah Shalom, my giver of peace; Jehovah-Rophe, our healer; Jehovah Lsidkenu, our righteousness; Jehovah Shammah, ever present one; Jehovah Rohi, our Good Shepherd. Also my parents reminded me that without faith in God it is impossible to please Him when confronted with life's barricades of hatred.

The book of James reaffirmed my parent's teachings about the significance of preserving your peace and joy while standing on the promises of God even when you are faced with trials and tribulations. James underscored the importance of prayer and supplication, patience and having faith in God and He would do just what He promised. James 5: 10-13 (KJV), *Take, my brethren, the prophets, who have spoken in the name of the Lord, for example of suffering affliction, and of patience. Behold, we count them happy which endure. You have heard of the patience of Job, and have seen the end of the Lord; that the Lord is very pitiful, and of tender mercy. But above all things, my brethren, swear not, neither by heaven, neither by the earth, neither by any other oath: but let your yes be yes; and your no, no; lest you fall into condemnation. Is any among you afflicted? Let him pray. Is any merry? Let him sing psalms.*

I firmly believe, once we afford the enemy an opportunity to steal our peace and happiness, it's merely a matter of time before we allow our flesh to shift into over drive and consume us with anger, frustration and vengeance. As a result, our spiritual compass is no longer able to navigate our walk of faith and we are inevitably thrown off course and left to fight with our own fleshly might and power.

However, John brought to my remembrance, when he heard Jesus explaining how He was able to manifest Himself to the disciples and not to the world in John 14: 26-28, (KJV), *But the Comforter, which is the Holy Ghost, whom the Father will send in My name, He shall teach you all things, and bring all things to your remembrance, whatsoever I have said to you. Peace I leave with you, My peace I give unto you: not as the world gives, give I unto you. Let not your heart be troubled, neither let it be afraid. You have heard how I said to you, I go away, and come again to you. If you loved Me, you would rejoice, because I said, I go to the Father: for My Father is greater than I.*

Once you understand how important it is to solely rely on God during your walk through the valley of the shadow of employment discrimination, you will better appreciate the choice of selecting the rugged road towards truth, honesty, purity, love, kindness, meekness and of a good report opposed to the dark smooth alleys of deceit, evil, corruption, selfishness, arrogance, greed, hatred, jealousy, enviousness, and absolute power which corrupts absolutely.

Once you understand how important it is to solely rely on God during your walk through the valley of the shadow of employment discrimination, you can no longer continue to hide as a Christian beneath the dark covers of silence and ignore the atrocities experienced against your brothers and sisters in Christ by your fellow man and still be true to God.

Once you understand how important it is to solely rely on God during your walk through the valley of the shadow of employment discrimination, you will have a greater appreciation for the blood that was shed on behalf of our African American ancestors. They were forced to endure the dreadful journey of slavery and racial discrimination through the civil rights movement for our freedom.

Once you understand how important it is to solely rely on God during your walk through the valley of the shadow of employment discrimination, you will come to realize that it's not about winning against the injustices that plague our society in a test towards measuring victory, it's about standing up for what is right and allowing our light to shine in the midst of darkness so that God can get the glory.

Once you understand how important it is to solely rely on God during your walk through the valley of the shadow of employment discrimination, you can begin to "**SHOUT WITH A VICTORY**" because of the promise that God will reward them that diligently seek Him. God has all power in His hands and knows our ending before there was a beginning.

The same God that promised never to leave us nor forsake us; the same God that sits high and looks low; the same God that inspired the Psalm writer in Psalm 47: 1-8 (KJV), *O Clap your hands, all you people; shout to God with the voice of triumph. For the Lord Most High is awesome; He is a great King over all the earth. He shall subdue the people under us, and the nations under our feet. He shall choose our inheritance for us, the Excellency of Jacob whom He loved. God is gone up with a shout, the Lord with the sound of a trumpet. Sing praises to God, sing praises: sing praises to our King, sing praises. For God is the King of all the earth: sing you praises with understanding. God reigns over the heathen: God sits upon the throne of His holiness.*

Therefore, I would like to encourage my brothers and sisters in Christ to **"SHOUT WITH A VICTORY"** during your walk through the valley of the shadow of employment discrimination. Let the world know that God never fails and begin singing a song of praise like the Psalm writer in Psalm 100:1-5 (KJV), *Make a joyful noise to the Lord, all you lands, serve the Lord with gladness: come before His presence with singing. Know you that the Lord He is God: it is He that has made us, and not we ourselves; we are His people, and the sheep of His pasture. Enter into His courts with praise: be thankful to Him, and bless His name. For the Lord is good; His mercy is everlasting; and His truth endures to all generations.*

In the event you happen to become overjoyed with the Holy Spirit while listing to a psalm of praise, I encourage you to allow the Psalm writer to walk with you on the remaining journey, since you already know the rest of the story. He will remind us why we still need to **"SHOUT WITH A VICTORY"** despite our circumstances in Psalm 34: 1-4 (KJV), *I will bless the Lord at all times: His praise shall continually be in my mouth. My soul shall make her boast in the Lord: the humble shall hear thereof, and be glad. O magnify the Lord with me, and let us exalt His name together. I sought the Lord, and He heard me, and delivered me from all my fears.* ***"AND ALL OF GOD'S CHILDEN SAID, AMEN."***

CONCLUSION

The Boiling Pot of Injustice: Wounded by Cowardice appeals to Christians to have faith and to help one another experiencing employment discrimination. It should encourage churches and various grass roots organizations to work together and stand against the powers of injustice. This collaborative effort will mandate accountability and build a spiritual force by providing a beacon of hope for those employees who have no where to run during their journey of employment discrimination. Therefore, I appeal to everyone to conduct a self examination of themselves and ask the following two questions: if they had to encounter employment discrimination and were in need of assistance and guidance, would they feel relieved to know that those sent to help them were only permitted to use as much effort as they themselves demonstrated over the course of their professional careers to help others in their time of need? As a result, would your efforts have been enough to see you through your storm of discrimination?

As a Christian, I realized regardless of my tarnished reputation, emotional scars, and the church folk constantly questioning my motives, I had to remain focused on my conviction and listen to the voice of the Lord and stand up for what was right. The Apostle Paul encouraged me when he said in Romans 8:34-39, (KJV), *Who shall separate us from the love of Christ? Shall tribulation, or distress, or persecution, or famine, or nakedness, or peril, or sword? As it is written, FOR THY SAKE WE ARE KILLED ALL THE*

DAY LONG; WE ARE ACCOUNTED AS SHEEP FOR THE SLAUGHTER. Nay, in all these things we are more than conquerors through him that loved us. For I am persuaded, that neither death, nor life, nor angels, nor principalities, nor powers, nor things present, nor things to come, nor height, nor depth, nor any other creature, shall be able to separate us from the love of God, which is in Christ Jesus our Lord.

I thank the Lord for always squeezing my hand to remind me who ultimately was in control. Often times, I lost my way and focused on the unjust strides that were made against me by an organized system determined to silence me and destroy my reputation. Nevertheless, the Lord always managed to appear and grant me the peace that surpassed all understanding when I could not see my way through my circumstance. The Lord reminded me that it was not by my might, nor by my power the situation would be resolved, but through his Holy Spirit. As a result, I had to submit to the Lord and stop trying to fight the enemy on my own volition. As Christians we have a tendency to say, "Lord, I'll take it from here" and miss our blessing because we are determined to seek retribution opposed to allowing the Lord to fight our battles for us.

The main purpose of the Boiling Pot of Injustice: Wounded by Cowardice is to enlighten Christians of the constant struggles that employees encounter all over this world. Also, appeal to the churches to assume their rightful place as a voice of spiritual reason and authority within the midst of wickedness in high places.

Unfortunately, many churches have exchanged their spiritual fortitude for thirty pieces of faith base grant dollars to help God fund their building programs. Therefore, many of the churches find themselves in a precarious position by compromising their access to funds granted by "Pharaoh" and closing their eyes to the injustice that plagues the children of God. This certificate of prostitution assures the organized establishment a lifetime warranty of silence from the church community. As a result, the church becomes voiceless and the employee's facing discrimination can become helpless as they pursue their struggle for equality, justice and fairness.

On the other hand, I would like to thank God for those churches that take care of God's children not only by preaching the gospel, but feeding the hungry, clothing the naked, comforting the elderly, visiting the sick and those in prison, and standing up for what is right regardless of the consequences. Matthew wrote in Matthew 25:40, (KJV), *And the King shall answer and say unto them, Verily I say unto you, Inasmuch as ye have done it unto one of the least of these my brethren, ye have done it unto me.*

It is my prayer "The Boiling Pot of Injustice:" Wounded by Cowardice serves as a witness and makes an appeal to those who have lost there way and know not the name of Jesus Christ. In the event you were curious to read the book and noticed I referenced some of your misdeeds towards others, it's still not too late to turn from your wicked ways and accept Jesus Christ as your Lord and personal Savior. The Apostle Paul wrote in Romans 3:23, (KJV) *For all have sinned, and come short of the glory of God.* However, Paul said in Romans 5:8 (KJV), *But God commendeth his love towards us, in that, while we were yet sinners, Christ died for us.* Because of God's love for us, the Apostle Paul also wrote these words in Romans 10:9, 13(KJV), *That if thou shalt confess with thy mouth the Lord Jesus, and shalt believe in thine heart that God hath raised him from the dead, thou shalt be saved. (13) FOR WHOSOEVER SHALL CALL UPON THE NAME OF THE LORD SHALL BE SAVED.* As a result, the Apostle Paul concluded by saying in Romans 5:1, (KJV), *Therefore being justified by faith; we have peace with God through our Lord Jesus Christ.*

I close by referencing this statement many of the preacher's say during the alter call time as they appeal for those seeking prayer, membership, rededication and renewing a personal relationship with God or accepting Jesus Christ as your personal Lord and Savior, **"Won't You Come, And Give God Your Heart And The Preacher Your Hand."**

Let the all God's children say, **A-Men**.

SUMMARY

The Boiling Pot of Injustice was inspired as a result of my personal experience of racial discrimination and retaliation within a governmental system that ruled with arrogance and absolute power. As an African American Christian man, the results of my personal journey of filing a lawsuit against my employer altered my personal and professional life forever. The harsh reality of racial discrimination and retaliation force me to test my faith in God as I walked through the valley of the shadow of employment discrimination.

I felt compelled to retrace my steps and recount the painful discriminatory process in hopes of helping others should they be forced to deal with such an encounter within the workplace. Regardless of the trials and tribulations that await those of us who choose to stand against discrimination and injustice within the workplace, the Lord will grant the ultimate victory to them that have suffered afflictions for His name sake. Therefore, despite the worldly gains of discrimination, **"Shout with a Victory"** and begin singing a song of praise while relying on the promises of Christ.

BIOGRAPHY

Kelvin Bodley was born in Youngstown Ohio in 1962 to the proud parents of Rev. Dr. Simon & Jenny Bodley and is one of five children, Chenita, Lemoyne, Jackie and Gloria. Kelvin is a native of Chicago, Illinois and relocated to Orlando, Florida in 1994. In April of 2005, Kelvin accepted a position as Special Assistant to Mayor Anthony Grant, Town of Eatonville, the first African American incorporated and oldest municipality in America. As an architect of change, Kelvin plays a substantial role as an advocate for social change and is committed to assisting the Mayor with countless special projects that enhance neighborhood economic development and community empowerment.

As of March 1, 2006, Kelvin aspired to become an author and completed his first book entitled, "The Boiling Pot of Injustice" in an effort to encourage Christians to allow their light to shine as they walk through their valley of shadow of employment discrimination. Kelvin felt God inspired him to walk this journey of faith and sound the trumpet and educate Christians on the harsh reality of fighting against an organized system inundated with racial discrimination and hatred. Kelvin plans to travel across the country to organize churches and social organizations to stand in the gap for the least of God's children that cannot defend themselves against the discriminatory practices and spiritual wickedness in high places within the workplace.

In 1986 Kelvin graduated from the College of Business and Administration at Chicago State University with a

Bachelor of Science degree. Kelvin had a passion for social justice and furthered his education in 1998 and received his Masters degree in the field of Public Administration from the University of Central Florida.

Kelvin is a Minister of the Gospel under the leadership of Bishop Woody E. Freeman & Elder Ella Freeman at Full Deliverance Church of Jesus, Orlando, Florida. Kelvin is President and CEO of Fairness Ministries and has devoted his life to serving the Lord and fighting for social change for all of God's children regardless of race, gender or creed.

ADVERTISEMENT

The "Trumpet" has sounded, there is a battle going on and the workplace is the battlefield. The good news is you can take a stand because God is fighting on your side! In this powerful new book, Kelvin Bodley shares from his own experiences battling against discrimination in the workplace to show you how to triumph using God's unfailing provisions.

Printed in the United States
54146LVS00002BA/1-180